Endorsements for *Raised?*

In an easy-to-read and engaging, polite style, Dodson and Watson share personal stories and beliefs that highlight the importance of the resurrection of Jesus. If you have doubts about the resurrection of Jesus, I strongly encourage you to read and ponder this book! It will challenge you without scolding you and exhort you without condescension.

J. D. Payne, Ph.D., minister, professor, author, blogger

No historical events have had a greater impact on Western history and culture than the crucifixion and resurrection of Jesus Christ. Hundreds of books have been written about this, but *Raised?* is strikingly different. It takes doubt seriously, situates the resurrection in a grander biblical narrative, and clarifies meanings of words that are so often misunderstood. The subject matter of *Raised?* makes this book important, but the approach taken by Dodson and Watson is what makes it all matter. Read it expectantly!

Jonathan Merritt, author of *Jesus is Better
Than You Imagined*

Short books are most helpful when they get right to the heart of the issue … and of the reader. *Raised*? is one of those books. It demonstrates why the bodily resurrection of Jesus is believable and the difference his life makes in your own life. Read it and then share that life with others.

Gerry Breshears, profess
at Wester

D0670740

As an advocate of religious literacy, I encourage Christians *and* non-Christians alike to read this book. Christianity is the largest religion on the planet, and the Christian faith hinges on the seemingly implausible claim of the resurrection of Christ. Provocative, illuminating, and succinct, *Raised?* invites doubt and provokes faith by blending historical context and pastoral insight. Even if you don't accept the resurrection as truth, you will come away with a deeper understanding of the faith of more than two billion people.

> Eileen Flynn, former religion reporter
> for Austin *American-Statesman* and journalism
> and religion lecturer at the University of Texas

Dodson and Watson do a wonderful job demonstrating both the *plausibility* of the resurrection of Jesus and the *possibilities* for a life of hope that emerges from this world-transforming event. Highly recommended.

> Sean McDonough is professor of New Testament at Gordon-Conwell Theological Seminary and author of *Christ as Creator: Origins of a New Testament Doctrine.*

Raised?

Finding Jesus by Doubting the Resurrection

JONATHAN K. DODSON
& BRAD WATSON

ZONDERVAN

Raised?
Copyright © 2014 by Jonathan Dodson and Brad Watson

This title is also available as a Zondervan ebook.
Visit www.zondervan.com/ebooks.

Requests for information should be addressed to:

Zondervan, *Grand Rapids, Michigan 49530*

ISBN: 978-0-310-51735-1

Published in association with Yates & Yates, www.yates2.com.

Cover design: Ptarmak, Inc.
Interior design: David Conn

Printed in the United States of America

14 15 16 17 18 19 20 21 22 /DCI/ 20 19 18 17 16 15 14 13 12 11 10 9 8 7 6 5 4 3 2

This book is a collaborative work by Jonathan Dodson and Brad Watson. We are friends who both pastor in progressive, countercultural cities of Austin and Portland. We wrote this book out of our love for skeptics and respect for the questions they help us ask. We also write as believers who oscillate in real belief in the resurrected Christ. We hope it proves to be an insightful, stirring reflection on the resurrection. Jonathan worked primarily on chapters 1 and 3 and Brad contributed to chapters 2 and 4.

Contents

CHAPTER 1

Doubting
the Resurrection

And when they saw him they worshiped him, but some doubted.

—Matthew 28:17

One out of every five Americans does not believe in a deity. The "none" category in religious polls has doubled over the past ten years, and less than half of the population attends religious services on a regular basis.[1] As statistics rise on the decline of Christian faith in America, you may find yourself wondering if Christianity is really worth believing. After all, the Christian faith makes some audacious claims.

AUDACIOUS CLAIMS OF THE GOSPEL

Some of Christianity's most audacious claims are made right at the center of the faith — the gospel of Jesus Christ.

Though particulars vary, the gospel is something all Christians agree on: "that Christ died for our sins in accordance with the Scriptures, that he was buried, that he was raised on the third day" (1 Corinthians 15:3–4). At first glance, the *death* of Jesus of Nazareth is easy enough to embrace. While there has been considerable debate over the so-called "historical Jesus," it is beyond dispute that Jesus existed in history. It is also well documented that the Roman authorities crucified people regularly, and in fact, Jewish historian Josephus documented Jesus' death.[2] What ruffles feathers is the God-sized claim beneath his self-sacrifice. Jesus asserted his death was necessary for humanity. His insistence that we all need an atoning representative troubles our dignity. Jesus represented all of us? What gives him the right? Who says we need a representation or sacrifice anyway?

The bull's-eye of the gospel is the death *and resurrection* of Jesus. We don't have to dive deep to surface doubt regarding the resurrection. Its surface value is, well, *incredible*. The notion that a first-century Jewish man, crucified between two common criminals, was actually God and rose from the dead is hard to believe. In our experience, people don't beat death, especially after being in a grave for three days. In light of recent horror trends, we might be more inclined to believe in a zombie emerging from the dead than a resurrected and fully restored person. Yet, at the center of historic Christian faith is the belief that a Jewish man named Jesus was "raised."

If you doubt the resurrection, I'm glad. Anything worth

believing has to be worth questioning, but don't let your questions slip away unanswered. Don't reduce your doubts to a state of unsettled cynicism. Wrestle with your doubts. Find answers.[3] If you call yourself a believer, don't settle for pat proofs, emotional experiences, or duty-driven religion. Keep asking questions. Those who haven't questioned their faith can easily become doctrinaire, even detached from the everyday struggle of faith.

Whether you are a skeptic, believer, or somewhere in between, press into your doubt or push back on your faith. Question your faith and question your doubts. Determine good reasons for believing or not believing in the resurrection of Jesus Christ. If he really did defeat death, it changes everything. Doubt well and you can walk away from skepticism, cynicism, or blind faith into intellectual security, perceptive belief, and deeper commitment. You can know that you have honestly doubted the resurrection.

OTHERS WHO STRUGGLE TO BELIEVE

If you struggle with belief in the resurrection, you're in good company. The story of the resurrection includes many doubters—Jesus' friends, contemporary Greeks and Romans, and countless Jews. In order to doubt well, we will examine the suspicions of each of these groups. As we do, let's climb into the story to get our facts straight.

The resurrection story is rooted in a historical account of

events surrounding Jesus of Nazareth in first-century Palestine (modern-day Israel). Three of Jesus' disciples and one doctor turned historian, Luke, wrote the Gospels: Matthew, Mark, Luke, and John. They report these events from four different vantage points, narrating the life, ministry, death, and alleged resurrection of Jesus. These various perspectives on the gospel story make it difficult for some to find the Gospels reliable.

Yet, to be fair, we rarely bring this same criticism to a story that is reported differently in several newspapers. Why? Because we innately realize that *different* people capture *different* (and similar) details in any given happening. These varying perspectives and reports can actually enrich our understanding if they are read together. Moreover, discrepancy in accounts does not render an event mythical. For instance, historians frequently note there are two conflicting accounts of Hannibal's crossing the Alps. Yet, no historian questions the historicity of Hannibal's crossing. Without getting bogged down into too much detail, I will bring these perspectives together to summarize the resurrection story. While much more can be said on the reliability of the Gospels, I will leave that to more qualified scholars.[4]

A Skeptical Account of the Resurrection

The gospel authors tell us that Jesus predicted his death and resurrection years before it occurred (see, for example, John 2:22). Apparently, Jesus knew a torturous death was coming, and he moved toward it—not away from it. He was arrested in the evening as he met with his disciples in a garden to pray. Suddenly, he was interrupted by clanging armor and flaming torches. Roman soldiers moved in to arrest him at the behest of religious leaders (the Pharisees and Sadducees), who charged Jesus with sedition, a dangerous accusation in the Roman Empire.

How did the soldiers know where to find Jesus? Unflatteringly, the gospel writers include a subplot of betrayal. Judas, one of Jesus' twelve key disciples, sold his master out to the authorities for about a month's salary. As the soldiers and traitor approached, Jesus' disciples scattered, leaving him to face trial alone. Jesus was quickly tried in the early, predawn hours of Friday morning and then crucified on a Roman cross that afternoon. He was buried that same night in a borrowed grave.

On Sunday, after the Jewish Sabbath, two women visit Jesus' tomb to pay their respects and anoint his body with oils. Not knowing how they will remove the large stone from the tomb when they arrive, they are shocked to find his tomb uncovered and the stone rolled away. One of the gospel writers, Matthew, tells us that a dazzling white angel appeared, accompanied by an earthquake, to remove the stone. The two Marys meet the angel, who disarms some of their fears and doubts when he says to them: "Do not be afraid, for I know that you seek Jesus who was crucified. He is not here, for he has risen, as he said. Come, see the place where he lay"

(Matthew 28:5 – 7). Anticipating their disbelief, the angel guides them to see the proof — the tomb is empty!

The women believe the witness of the angel, who reminds them of the words Jesus had spoken just a few days earlier: "The Son of Man must suffer many things and be rejected by the elders and chief priests and scribes, and be killed, and on the third day be raised" (Luke 9:22). Their faith refreshed, the women return to tell the remaining eleven disciples.

What happens next is intriguing. As the women report seeing the resurrected Christ, their story is met with scorn: "These words seemed to [the disciples] an idle tale, and they did not believe [the women]" (Luke 24:11). When they hear the claim that Jesus has risen from the dead, they think it is idle talk, foolishness. They do not believe. They question. Hearing the report, they don't rubber-stamp the claim in blind faith. They respond like you and I would — skeptically. No wishful thinking here. They doubt. Impetuous Peter runs on ahead to see for himself. They question. Their faith is tested. And the doubting has only just begun.

As the report of Jesus' missing body spreads, people begin to wonder what has happened to it. Some claim the body was stolen. Even Mary Magdalene, a close follower of Jesus, assumes this until Jesus appears to her. Mary is feeling defeated by the death of her beloved teacher and is distraught to find his body missing. In her grief and confusion, she mistakes Jesus for a gardener. His voice doesn't register, not until he calls her by her name (John 20:15 – 16).

Mary isn't alone in her disbelief. Others struggle to believe her resurrection report, even *after* Jesus appears to them (Luke 24:36 – 43). His followers mistake him for a ghost, so Jesus proves his physical existence by eating a piece of fish before their very eyes, and they all believe, except Thomas. The Gospel of John informs us that Thomas was not present with the rest of the disciples when Jesus first appeared to the group. As a result, the disciples report their thrilling experience of the risen Christ to Thomas, who is incredulous. He insists on proof for this audacious claim: "Unless I see in his hands the mark of the nails, and place my finger into the mark of the nails, and place my hand into his side, I will never believe" (John 20:25).

In response, Christians have derided Thomas for his demand for evidence, calling him a pessimist and double-minded. But who can blame him? After all, didn't the other disciples get to see the risen Christ before coming to certain conviction? Thomas critics will be quick to point out his stubborn insistence that he not only see but also touch Christ, and not just his body, but his wounds as well. Obstinate skeptic! But aren't you glad there was someone there who didn't just take the word on the street, someone who valued proof, someone who knew that the wounds couldn't be faked? I am.

Put yourself in Thomas's shoes. If you had spent every day with Jesus for roughly the last one thousand days, knew his mannerisms, loved the timbre of his voice, embraced his teachings, seen his miracles, and wept at his death, and then heard from trusted friends that Jesus had risen from the dead, proving that he is not a spirit, wouldn't you be a bit skeptical? You might even demand proof. But what if Jesus appears right in front of you, and then, without a word, he quotes your earlier demands back to you: "Then he said to Thomas, 'Put your finger here, and see my hands; and put out your hand, and place it in my side. Do not disbelieve, but believe'" (John 20:27). Then you might quiver, perhaps even cower, like a child expecting a stern parental rebuke. How would you expect Jesus to respond?

Now, put yourself in the shoes of Jesus. You've spent all this time with Thomas, poured out your soul to him, prayed relentlessly for him, taught him numerous times about your impending death and resurrection, and then he doubts you, even *after* the other ten disciples have assured him of your resurrection and seen you eat a fish. Do you think your patience would run a little thin? I know mine would. I expect Jesus to rebuke Thomas, making him an example for everyone else, telling him to accept it and get with the program.

But that's not what Jesus does. Instead, Jesus has room for Thomas's doubt. He even invites Thomas to place his hands on his tender crucifixion wounds, to feel the truth. This scene is palpably human and curiously divine. We can identify with Thomas's response, but Jesus' tender patience is superhuman. In the History Channel's docudrama *The Bible*, this scene is touchingly captured with the resurrected Jesus slowly making his way over to Thomas, placing his hand gently on his shoulder, and saying: "Do not disbelieve, but believe" (John 20:27). Jesus has patience for doubt.

If you doubt the resurrection, you are in good company. Jesus understands your doubts, and he welcomes them. To those who are skeptical and struggling with belief, Jesus remains ready to receive your questions. He will listen to your doubts. He also implores belief, as he did with Thomas. He even extends a special grace to those who believe but have not seen him (John 20:29). Even so, you may still find yourself on the side of doubt. It is not easy to accept the notion that someone has risen from the dead. As a warm concession, some people embrace the historical Jesus, even admire his life example, but remain incredulous. The resurrection is a dividing line—a parting claim.

The resurrection is like a river that parts a road. People are on the road approaching the river. Arriving at the river of the resurrection, you look across it to where the road continues and see quite a few cars are parked there. In your doubt, you can't imagine how people got to the other side of the river. How did they get across? How can rational people come to the belief that Jesus died and rose from the dead?[5]

A Global Perspective

Truth be told, the parking lot on the other side of the resurrection is overflowing. Resurrection-believing Christians are all over the world. Today there are approximately 2.2 billion Christians in the world, almost a billion more Christians than

Muslims (who adhere to the world's second largest religion, Islam). Christians around the world claim a personal encounter with Christ and a relationship with a resurrected Jesus. Many of them are so devout they have suffered for their belief in the resurrected Christ. These believers come from a broad array of cultures and ethnic backgrounds. What are we to make of this? Are they all suffering from a mass delusion?

While Christianity is the world's largest (and most ethnically diverse) religion, is this reason enough to jump ship on your beliefs? Does the sheer number of believing, praying, suffering Christians make the resurrection true? No, not at all, but it should at least put it in the realm of *possibility*. Of course, we could also say the same thing about Islam. However, Muslims do not claim a resurrected messiah. Allah, the name for God in Islam, is not a God who suffers for humanity and conquers death. In Jesus, we see God crucified and raised to life. According to the Bible, the resurrection of Jesus is a preview of things to come (1 Corinthians 15).

The resurrection isn't restricted to Jesus either. All who have faith in him will eventually gain a resurrected body to enjoy a "resurrected" world. This is certainly a hopeful idea. And if billions of people and thousands of cultures have found hope in the resurrection, might there perhaps be something to it? After all, how did all those diverse people and ethnic groups come to believe a claim as implausible as the resurrection of Jesus?

Today, the majority of the Christian population has

shifted away from the West to the South and the East.[6] The current statistical-geographical center of global Christianity is, quite literally, Timbuktu, Mali.[7] That's Africa. The largest Christian nation is now China. It is worth noting that the current center of global Christianity is found among cultures that affirm the supernatural. Their worldviews don't automatically preclude supernatural events. In fact, people in the global South will tell you that they experience inexplicable, transrational events on a regular basis. This is not typical in the West, where we rule out the supernatural. We rarely see extraordinary things (or at least admit to them). Instead, we begin with the assumption that the supernatural is not possible.

Is this position truly open-minded? It certainly seems biased and closed off to possibilities we may not have personally experienced. Shouldn't we at least be open to the possibility of Jesus rising from the dead? In fact, many are willing to believe in the supernatural teachings of Buddha, Vishnu, and Eckhart Tolle, but what about Jesus? If we are to consider fairly the plausibility of the resurrection—whether it happened or not we must begin with its *possibility*. Possibility is the only intellectually honest place to begin. But let's not abandon critical thinking. Let's begin by taking a look at what other skeptics said, those who were alive at the time of Jesus' alleged resurrection. Did *they* find the resurrection plausible? How did some of them get across the river of doubt?

The Greeks

There were two major groups of skeptics around during the time of Jesus—Jews and Greeks.[8] Let's begin with the Greeks. For the most part, the Greeks were open to the supernatural. Although Greek philosophy evolved over time from Homeric belief in gods like Zeus to Plato's belief in philosophy like the Forms, the Greeks still believed there were forces greater than nature at work in the world. However, views of what happened at death varied. Some Greeks, like Homer, believed that a human being becomes a disembodied, witless spirit destined to roam Hades. You may remember the Underworld from high school mythology, a gloomy place of postmortem existence where souls roam in the shadows, devoid of sunlight. For Homerians, death was not a welcome prospect.

Other Greeks anticipated escape from the world at the point of death. The Epicureans believed the soul was composed of particles that disintegrated upon death. For them, there was no existence after death at all. Death was welcomed but not with the hope of life.

Those who followed Plato believed that the soul was immaterial and good. Upon death the soul was liberated from the body into a Hades altogether different. For Platonists, Hades was not a place of gloom but a place of delight, of extended philosophical discussion. In the thought of Plato, death was welcomed with the hope of escaping the body.

The three main views on the afterlife are summarized in this chart.

GREEKS AND THE AFTERLIFE

Homerians: death was not a welcome prospect.
Epicureans: death was welcomed but not with the hope of life.
Platonists: death was welcomed with the hope of escaping the body.

This brief summary of Greek views on the afterlife tells us at least one thing: *the idea of an embodied life after death, of a resurrection, was neither possible nor desirable.* The Greeks saw the world and the body as something prone to decay. When a person died, they were liberated from their body. The body was a cage. The band Arcade Fire captures this sentiment with Platonic spin: "My body is a cage that keeps me from dancing with the one I love / But my mind holds the key."[9]

For the Greeks, salvation was an escape from, not a renewal of, the body. And even if they had wanted a resurrection, which they did not, it was still an impossible idea. N. T. Wright helpfully summarizes: "The ancient world was thus divided into those who said that the resurrection couldn't happen, though they might have wanted it to, and those who said they didn't want it to happen, knowing that it couldn't happen anyway."[10] Today, Eastern religions such as Hinduism, Buddhism, and Taoism follow a similar line of thinking.

Death is seen as an escape from the body. The ancient Greeks possessed no hope of an embodied existence after death. Resurrection was not just implausible; it was undesirable.

How does this Hellenistic view of the afterlife relate to the Christian claim of the resurrection? If you were to tell a Greek man, "Jesus was just raised from the dead," he would probably scratch his head and say, "*Why* would he want to do that? *Why* would he want to return to his cage, to resume existence in this inferior, decaying world? Why not embrace the liberating power of death? To die is to be set free. Why would anyone *want* to be resurrected?" To put it simply, resurrection wasn't a positive, hopeful idea for the Greeks.

But the Greeks weren't the only ones to hear the claim of the resurrected Jesus. What about the other group of people who were alive during the alleged resurrection of Jesus? What did the Jews think?

The Jews

Unlike the Greeks, the Jews did believe in the resurrection of the body. The Hebrew Bible describes a great resurrection at the end of history, when everyone will be reunited with their bodies to stand before God for judgment and salvation (Ezekiel 37; Daniel 7). The prophet Daniel writes: "And many of those who sleep in the dust of the earth shall awake, some to everlasting life, and some to shame and everlasting contempt. And those who are wise shall shine like the brightness of the sky above; and those who turn many to righteousness, like the stars forever and ever" (Daniel 12:2–3). Shame and contempt are promised to those who do not submit to God, but to those who hope in YHWH (the Hebrew name for God, probably pronounced YAH-way), a bright and bodily future is promised.

For the Jews, resurrection was a desirable thing. Their faith in a Creator God led them to see the body as something worth preserving. Mankind was made in the image of God and instructed to "be fruitful and multiply and fill the earth" (Genesis 1:26–28). Desecrating this image, as in the case of Cain's murder of Abel, was wrong, and a matter for judgment. In contrast to the Greeks, the Hebrews believed the body was worth creating, preserving, *and* resurrecting.

We see hints of this in the Old Testament. We find several "death-resurrection" stories, such as the birth of Isaac from a "dead" womb, the escape of Joseph from near death in a pit and prison, the resuscitation of a widow's son, and Elijah's bodily departure from earth in a fiery chariot. Taken together, these stories are signs that physical, bodily resurrection is something hopeful and positive in Jewish culture.

Later Jewish literature continues to develop these themes.[11] This literature includes descriptions of resurrection and cosmic rebirth, where the righteous are "raised up" and the corrupt die (*4 Ezra* 8:31). The Qumran community, responsible for the Dead Sea Scrolls, describes a future messianic kingdom that is characterized by peace, joy, rest, health, and even immortality (*2 Apocalypse of Baruch* 73:1–3). Referring to an end-time resurrection event, the prophet Ezekiel remarks: "Thus says the LORD God: Behold, I will open your graves and raise you from your graves, O my people. And I will bring you into the land of Israel" (Ezekiel 37:12). Ezekiel describes that land as a rehabilitated garden of Eden, where cities flourish and the wastelands are rebuilt.

Tied to the bodily resurrection is also the idea that the world will be renewed and restored to its state of wholeness as a garden paradise. In other words, this is a universal promise. The bodily resurrection isn't just getting new bodies; it involves the renewal of what has been destroyed — cities, the land, and all of creation (Isaiah 60; Ezekiel 36). For the Jews, bodily resurrection was seen as a cosmic, one-time event that would occur at the end of history. The end of the world would bring about a resurrected creation.

Now, you may be thinking, "Sounds interesting, but what does all of this have to do with whether or not Jesus was raised from the dead?" A lot! If you approached a Jewish woman in the first century and told her Jesus was her Messiah and that he had just been raised from the dead, she would look at you in consternation and ask why. After all, we've seen that Jews believe resurrection is possible — even something good, a hopeful future. The reason they would find the resurrection of Jesus unbelievable is because the *timing* and *scope* of the resurrection would be off.

Like the Greeks, Jews would scratch their heads and say: "Are you crazy? Look around; it's not the end of history. I don't have a new body, we are still suffering, the world is still broken, and the Romans still oppress us. All things have not been made new." *For Jews, it was unthinkable that resurrection would occur in the middle of history, apart from worldwide renewal of the created order.* The timing would be wrong. Even more unthinkable was the idea that a single *individual* would be resurrected rather than all humanity at once. Limiting the scope of the resurrection to a single person would be inconceivable.

What should we conclude from these first-century skeptics? Both Jews *and* Greeks living at the time of Christ would have found the resurrection of Jesus implausible. Both groups would have scratched their heads and wondered how in the world anyone would come up with such a crazy idea. To return to our analogy of crossing the river dividing belief from unbelief — they'd wonder how anyone could get across the river. So, if you find the resurrection a bit crazy, know that you're in good company! Centuries of Greek and Jewish thought agree with you.

So what do we conclude? Are they right? If the Greeks and the Jews had good reasons to think the resurrection didn't make sense, what are we to conclude really happened on Easter morning?

WHAT REALLY HAPPENED EASTER MORNING?

Consider this. In the first century, Greeks and Jews who possessed age-old beliefs — deep convictions affecting the

way they saw themselves and the world around them—
suddenly changed their beliefs to embrace the resurrection.
On a dime, they converted to faith in a resurrected Christ.
Why? How are we to account for this sudden and dramatic
shift in their beliefs? Suddenly, thousands and thousands of
Jews and Greeks become Christians. It's unthinkable!

For some, this shift in their beliefs was instant! Centuries of philosophy and theology drastically changed in a
few short years. Acclaimed biblical scholar N. T. Wright
points out that this kind of theological change typically
takes decades, if not longer, to occur. Unexpectedly, these
men and women now believed that life after death was possible, not in an abstract way, but because of a belief about
a specific historical person, Jesus of Nazareth. Overnight,
they came to believe that Jesus had risen from the dead.
What accounts for this radical worldview shift that happened virtually overnight?

We should note that we are not alone in asking these
questions. Historians and scholars have also been puzzled
by this phenomenon and have sought to come up with a
good explanation.

Was It a Delusion?

If you assume that the resurrection could not have happened, the next best explanation is that this sudden shifting of beliefs was the result of a mass delusion. In other
words, thousands of people who believed that Jesus had

risen from the dead and changed their lives *must* have been deluded. One problem with this explanation is that the early Christians didn't *act* delusional. Delusional people often withdraw from society. That didn't happen. When other citizens abandoned the cities to escape plagues and sickness, the early Christians remained behind to tend to the sick. Instead of withdrawing from society, they became more involved, seeking to make life better. In his critical work on early Christianity, scholar Rodney Stark remarks:

> Religion did not merely offer psychological antidotes for the misery of life; it actually made life less miserable. The power of Christianity lay not in its promise of otherworldly compensations for suffering in this life, as has so often been proposed. The truly revolutionary aspect of Christianity lay in moral imperatives such as "Love one's neighbor as one's self," "Do unto others as you would have them do unto you," "It is more blessed to give than to receive," and "When you did it to the least of my brethren, you did it to me." These were not just slogans. Members did nurse the sick, even during epidemics; they did support orphans, widows, the elderly, and the poor.[12]

The early Christians were more than just another eccentric cult. They were a compassionate people. And their love and compassion was rooted in what they believed. Because of the resurrection, they had every reason to care for their neighbors. Unlike Greek philosophy, the Christian faith affirmed the body as worthy of resurrection, worthy of care. This naturally led them to care for the sick and hurting.

Jesus did not rise from the dead as a spirit or try to escape from his body, as if it were a cage. Rather, he emerged from the grave in a renewed, physical body. His postmortem wounds reinforced his corporeal existence. According to the Gospels, the person the disciples saw was real, flesh and bone.

The resurrection affirms the value of the human body. We will look at the implications of all this more closely in chapter 4, but at the very least it shows us that the early Christians weren't delusional. Crazy people don't care for others at their own expense.

Witnessing the Resurrection

If belief in the resurrection wasn't a mass delusion—and we know that thousands of Greeks and Jews did, in fact, abandon their long-held beliefs—what accounts for this radical social and cultural shift? *The only believable explanation is that they actually witnessed the resurrected Christ or heard from someone who saw Jesus in resurrected form.* Why else would they contradict theology passed down for thousands of years? Why run the risk of cultural scorn and familial rejection?

Perhaps it would be helpful to draw upon an analogy at this point. Think of the staunchest Republican or Democrat you know. They know their political platform backward and forward. They put signs in their yard for their candidates and bumper stickers on their cars, volunteer for party campaigns, proselytize others with their political convictions, blow up social media with their views, and never miss an opportunity to vote. Now, imagine that person suddenly switching parties. In an instant, they reverse their views on foreign policy, government, health care, same-sex marriage, gun control, and abortion. The Republican becomes a Democrat overnight; the Democrat goes Republican.

Unthinkable, right? *It was equally unthinkable for Jews and Greeks to change their views regarding the resurrection.* To shift from thinking the body is bad and worthy of escape to believing that the body is good and worthy of resurrection was inconceivable to Greeks. To conceive of a resurrection in the middle of history, limited to one man, was preposterous for the Jews. The only believable explanation for this sudden shift is that people actually witnessed the resurrected Christ.

Think about it. If you met and conversed with someone you knew had died, wouldn't your beliefs and views change? Now, what if this person also claimed to be God, possessing the power to forgive your sins and grant you eternal life? You know that there will be consequences to going public with your beliefs. Friends will avoid you. Family members will no longer invite you to holiday parties, or worse, they will reject and disown you. Neighbors will scorn you. If you are living in the first century, the Roman government will oppose you and Emperor Nero will burn you to death.

So why run the risk of social marginalization and personal sacrifice if Jesus did *not* rise from the dead? The first

Christians must have experienced something so convincing that they were willing to follow Jesus' teachings, no matter the cost. They claim to have witnessed the resurrected Christ. The Gospel writers and the apostle Paul attest: "He was buried ... raised on the third day in accordance with the Scriptures, and ... he appeared to Cephas [Peter], then to the twelve. Then he appeared to more than five hundred brothers at one time" (1 Corinthians 15:4–6). Hundreds of people, men and women, witnessed the resurrected Christ with their own eyes, and they found they couldn't keep that experience to themselves. In fact, two other staunch skeptics did an about-face on their views regarding Jesus. Skeptical journalist Lee Strobel writes: "Then we have two skeptics who regarded Jesus as a false prophet: Paul, the persecuter of the church and James, who was Jesus' half-brother. They changed their opinions 180 degrees after encountering the risen Jesus."[13]

The death and resurrection of Jesus weren't events that happened in a private corner of the world. They were public events, on display for many to see and investigate. There was no reason for the disciples to invent this idea; it went against the grain of Roman politics, Jewish theology, and Greek ideals. The only plausible explanation is that these witnesses were telling and recording the truth of what they had seen, namely, that Jesus of Nazareth was not only crucified and buried but also raised from the dead. They changed their beliefs because they witnessed the death-defeating Jesus and found his testimony life-altering.

Jews became Christians as they heard the story that the resurrection had begun in the middle of history, starting with Jesus. Old Testament stories made sense in a new way, clicking into place. Prophecies were fulfilled, albeit earlier than expected. Greeks suddenly believed, not only in life after death, but also that bodily life after death was good—that the body was not a cage; it was, instead, a precious gift. People found their lives now packed with meaning. They felt compelled to care for the lame, the poor, and the needy. The resurrection—literally—changed everything for them.

If you struggle to believe the resurrection, you're not all that different than most of the Jews and Greeks who lived in Jesus' day. The resurrection of a man from the dead was not easy to believe then, nor is it easy to accept today. It has never been easy to believe—and yet millions have.

If you still don't believe it, it's understandable. It's difficult to switch beliefs overnight. Doubt is normal—even good.[14] But at some point you've got to come up with an explanation for this massive shift in belief, the hundreds of eyewitnesses, and the detailed history of these events recorded in the Gospels. If after that you still don't believe—you can't bring yourself to believe it is true—I'm going to suggest that *you should want to believe it is true*.[15] Why? Because the resurrection changes everything. There are implications that follow what we believe. If the resurrection is true, it means that people aren't witless spirits or meaningless series of biological mutations. They are made in the image of God and worth resurrecting. And that's good news.

As we wrap up this first chapter, I'd like to share a way the resurrection changed my life.

WHY YOU SHOULD WANT THE RESURRECTION TO BE TRUE

I lost my best friend in college. Chris died of a gunshot to the head. I'll never forget the moment I first heard the news. I was walking into my apartment after a long road trip and found a massive number of people crowded in my living room. A morose, mysterious mood hung in the air. I immediately sensed they all knew something I didn't.

"Sit down, I need to tell you something," said a friend.

"No, I'll stand. What is it?" I replied.

I'll never forget the next few words. "Chris has been shot; he's in the hospital in Dallas."

I don't remember much after that. Just before midnight, I hit the road for Dallas with my brother, aware that I could potentially lose my best friend sometime in the next three and a half hours as we drove. During that drive, I oscillated from fear, to grief, to prayer, to depressing thoughts about a future without Chris. Death had come knocking, and I hated the sound. At 3:00 a.m., we finally reached the hospital. It was annoyingly bright when we entered, and I went straight to Chris' parents to talk with them and get an update. "It's not good," they said. "We're going to have to pull the life support. He is brain dead."

I walked into the room and saw a bloated, lifeless version of my best friend. One look at the body lying in the bed, and I knew it was Chris. I recognized him, but I didn't. It was a strange experience. The person in the bed looked like Chris, but somehow I knew that he wasn't fully there anymore.

The New Testament teaches that our spirit goes to be with our Creator when we die until Christ returns to resurrect our bodies and make all things new (Revelation 20:5, 11 – 15). Faith in a resurrected Christ gives us hope that Jesus' resurrection was just the first of many future resurrections yet to come. To experience this resurrection, we must abandon faith in ourselves and put our faith in Jesus' death and resurrection. Chris had done this. His generous, kind-hearted, Christlike life reflected it. When we give up on faith in self and instead put faith in the risen Christ, we experience a death and resurrection of our own, a spiritual resurrection that will one day culminate in a bodily resurrection. Jesus defeats sin and death to give us, through his Spirit, a new life that is both spiritual and physical (Romans 8:10 – 11). In Jesus, there is hope for a true, imperishable resurrection body that will never die:

> For the trumpet will sound, and the dead will be raised imperishable, and we shall be changed. For this perishable body must put on the imperishable, and this mortal body must put on immortality. When the perishable puts

on the imperishable, and the mortal puts on immortality, then shall come to pass the saying that is written:

> "Death is swallowed up in victory."
> "O death, where is your victory?
> O death, where is your sting?"
> (1 Corinthians 15:52–55)

Although death is painful, the resurrection tells us that death does not have the final word. Those who hope in the death-defeater, Jesus, have the promise of life forever. Staring at Chris as he lay in that hospital bed, I was comforted by the promise that when his body would one day be reunited with his spirit, the two of us would experience a grand reunion. Not even death can end our friendship. One day there will be no more death, no bloated, lifeless corpse lying in a hospital bed. There will only be a new, bodily life together in a joyous new creation. My friend Chris is not condemned to wander Hades as a witless spirit for all eternity, as the Greeks believed. His life was, is, and will be full of meaning.

Sentiment Versus Hope

A lot of people share some of the sentiment behind what I'm saying, believing in some type of heaven.[16] It's common for people to offer empty platitudes around death: "We'll see him in the afterlife," or, "She's in a better place." What moves this from wishful sentiment to certain hope? While the resurrection certainly offers us a promise of life after death, the promise only extends to those who have hoped in the Resurrector. Jesus said: "I am the resurrection and the life. Whoever believes in me, though he die, yet shall he live, and everyone who lives and believes in me shall never die" (John 11:25–26). Notice—Jesus isn't talking about a generic truth for everyone. The "resurrection" is *in Christ*. To those who hope in Christ for resurrection life, gaining life after death with him makes sense.

But it's important to see the hope is not in gaining a resurrection body. While stunning, the new body isn't the final reward. Christ is the ultimate reward. Jesus Christ *is* the resurrection and the life—the most powerful, beautiful, creative person in the universe. When we believe in him, we gain a forever union with this stunning, amazing Person. This is why Paul can say, before death, "To live is Christ, and to die is gain" (Philippians 1:21). Paul already knew resurrection life with Christ, in a spiritual sense, and he looked forward to its consummation in a new physical body at some point in the future. The resurrection of the body is a blessing, a wonderful gift, that comes with Jesus.

Those who only have nice sentiments about heaven but do not have Christ have no real hope for resurrection. If they are honest with themselves, they aren't interested in being with Christ; they just want to avoid death or a painful existence after death. They have put their hope elsewhere, perhaps in things like familial love, career status, or being a good person. The sentimental person, then, is more likely to speak of their hope to be reunited with a loved one, rather than to talk of being with Love himself, Jesus. They do not want *the resurrection*, but a resurrection that shields them from the truth of death.

Sentiment is altogether different from hope; it is based on improving how we feel, not on what is real or true. Hope, however, is based on a promise. In this case, God himself makes the promise to us. As the resurrection and the life, Jesus binds himself, in this life and the next, to impart resurrection life to those who put their hope in him.

Believing in God's Promises

After Chris' funeral, I stopped by to see his parents again. They had kept three suicide notes—one to his family, one to his girlfriend, and one to me. The legal-size envelope was sealed and creased. I excused myself to open it in silence. With the door cracked, I sat down on the floral bed duvet and read in hopeful suspense:

"I'm sorry, bro. I know this isn't right, but I also know that He will never leave me or forsake me."

Chris was alluding to Hebrews 13:5: "Keep your life free from love of money, and be content with what you have, for he has said, 'I will never leave you nor forsake you.'" Despite his insane path to death, I could see that Chris had still held onto a sane hope in life. He wrote these words torn between two promises, one false and one true. The false one promised life in death, an escape. The true one promised life after death. In Christ, Chris had every reason to live.

But in the haze of his sufferings, Chris could not make out Christ clearly. Sentiment beckoned him toward death; hope pointed him to life. With the promise of death in one hand and the promise of Christ in the other, he pulled the trigger.

You and I face life and death choices every day. Like a river blocking our way forward, the resurrection is one of those choices—a matter of life or death. Is it possible to make it across the river, from unbelief to belief in the resurrection? For some, it seems impossible. But many find their way across. How? The same way the early Christians did, by an encounter with the risen Jesus.

This encounter isn't presently with a flesh-and-blood person. Though he will return an embodied Savior-King, our initial encounter with the risen Christ is by faith—but so was the disciples. Even his own disciples doubted him at first sight. Their sudden shift from unbelief to belief was sparked by faith in the promises of the risen Jesus. His disciple John tells us: "When therefore he was raised from the dead, *his disciples remembered that he had said this, and they believed the Scripture and the word that Jesus had spoken*" (John 2:22, italics added). The promises he spoke to them are good for us as well: "I am the resurrection and the life. Whoever believes in me, though he die, yet shall he live, and everyone who lives and believes in me shall never die" (John 11:25–26).

Faith is the unnoticed ferry, lying hidden near the bank of the river, that can take us from the riverbank of doubt, across the waters that divide, to the other side of belief in the resurrection. It's not blind faith, as some wrongly assume. You don't cross by closing your eyes and wishing Jesus' resurrection was true. No. You cross with your eyes wide open. This is an informed faith, faith in a historically plausible resurrection, attested by hundreds of witnesses, one proven to be worth believing. We will talk about the nature of faith in chapter 3.

For now, we hope you'll weigh what we've said, take some time to read (or reread) the Gospel accounts of Jesus, and turn in faith to the God who died our death and gave us his life so that we might have the promise of life *before* death and life *after* death, spiritual and physical. Will you believe and live a resurrected life? It makes all the difference in the world.

CHAPTER 2

How the Resurrection Reshapes History

Then [Jesus] said to them, "These are my words that I spoke to you while I was still with you, that everything written about me in the Law of Moses and the Prophets and the Psalms must be fulfilled." Then he opened their minds to understand the Scriptures, and said to them, "Thus it is written, that the Christ should suffer and on the third day rise from the dead."

—Luke 24:44–46

Y̲ou may still have doubts. We are expecting that. But let's say you are open to the possibility that perhaps Jesus was, indeed, raised from the dead. One question you might have is "Why?" What's the point of the resurrection? Is it just a way of getting attention? Was it meant to prove something? To get at the "why" of the resurrection, we need to consider it as part of a larger narrative—a bigger story. How does the seemingly nonsensical resurrection of Jesus make sense of the history of humanity? What is the greater story in which the resurrection takes place? We will unfold the biblical story to show how the resurrection reshapes history through four scenes:

- Creation of the World
- Fall from Perfect Relationship
- Redemption by Christ
- Renewed Future[17]

Each of these scenes has a central character that pushes the story along. There are twists and turns, substories and subplots that don't fit together like a contemporary novel or film would, but throughout the narrative we find common threads that tie the story together. There are three central characters in the narrative: Adam, Abraham, and Jesus. By looking at these characters we can make some sense of the unfolding story of the Bible, a story of life and death.

CREATION OF THE WORLD

In the beginning, God created the heavens and the earth (Genesis 1).[18] He made everything, and it was good. The world was a place of universal thriving, filled with rivers, animals, plants, and the crown of God's creation—humanity.

God is the first and primary character of the Bible, but after we are introduced to him, the next person we meet is a man named Adam. Adam is the first human being, created by God, and then followed by his wife, Eve. The first couple is given abundant provision for human flourishing. They have life and purpose.

Abundant Life

Imagine a world without disease, decay, or even death. Imagine having all the food, water, and shelter you need — forever. In addition to all of this, picture the perfect mate created and given to you. This was Adam's life. In fact, Adam breaks out singing over his new wife when he first sees her. At that time, they walked naked and lived in intimate relationship. Moreover, Adam and Eve had no shame — there was no blame shifting, fighting, or hurt feelings.

Adam and Eve also had a vibrant relationship with God. God walked with them in the cool of the day. He taught them how to live and enjoyed spending time with them. God even spoke directly with them. Adam and Eve were close friends of God. He was present in their lives. This is a picture of human life as it was intended to be, and this was the world that existed for the first two human beings. They were blessed.

Abundant Purpose

When God made Adam and Eve in his image, he blessed them and gave them a command: "Be fruitful and multiply and fill the earth and subdue it, and have dominion over the fish of the sea and over the birds of the heavens and over every living thing that moves on the earth" (Genesis 1:28). The command to "be fruitful and multiply" (make babies) and "subdue the earth" (make culture) was a blessing God gave to Adam and Eve. By making babies and culture, they would populate a perfect creation. This would result in human flourishing—the growth of rich relationships and a kaleidoscope of human culture for them to enjoy.

The future is bright—God dwelling with humanity in a perfect, trusting relationship. Adam and Eve are charged with spreading this rich relationship and creating culture in a way that reflects God's gracious, creative rule. To carry out this command, God furnishes them with everything they need: one another, a garden, communion with him, rule over the creatures, and a single prohibition—eat from any tree in the garden except for one.

FALL FROM PERFECT RELATIONSHIP

Adam and Eve had it all. God's blessing would continue as they lived in obedience to his gracious kingship. Then the wheels came off. Before this grand project had traveled far, the first humans disobeyed the single prohibition God had given to them. They didn't trust God; they failed to believe in his goodness, and they rejected the purpose he had given to them. This was no accident. They made a choice to distrust their trustworthy Creator, thinking they could carve out a life better than the one God had provided for them. They took matters into their own hands and flipped the created order—preferring the creature over the Creator.

The results were devastating. Immediately, they sensed shame at what they had done, and they hid from God and blamed one another. Their relationships were filled with discord. They sold out their benevolent Creator and his perfect intimacy and broke trust with one another. The blessing of God was withdrawn, and they were exiled from the garden.

What had been a blessing now became cursed. The responsibilities of childbirth and work (making babies and culture) became difficult to pursue. They encountered struggle in the process of childbearing and pursuing vocation, a struggle that continues to this day. Can you relate? If you have ever found it difficult to raise kids or have a strong, healthy marriage relationship, then you know the effects of this fall from grace. Have you ever found your work arduous and frustrating? This too is the consequence of the fall.

Pain, sweat, and death entered the world through our ancestors' disobedience. Murder and exploitation soon followed (Genesis 4; 6:1–8). Adam and Eve, the humans commissioned to spread life into the whole world, instead spread death. The hope of the world hung on Adam's obedience, and that hope came crashing down with his disobedience. Because of Adam's actions, future human relationship with God was utterly ruined. The dark hopelessness of death permeated the human story.

The Reverberations of Adam's Failure

Reverberations of Adam's failure have continued through history and the passing of time. Consider how the fall continues to impact relationships today.

Bob has never felt accepted or a sense of belonging. He went to an Ivy League school and owns a home in each of the most expensive zip codes in America. He divorced two wives and left three sons and a daughter behind. He has tried everything: adventurous vacations, expensive watches, and sexual pleasure. He spends most of his evenings in his Manhattan flat, lonely and self-absorbed.

Sheryl is rejected and alone. Abandoned at five, she was raised by grandparents who beat her and by uncles who abused her in horrific ways. She was continually told she wasn't smart. She cheated her way through an Associates degree, while every man she slept with cheated on her.

Togo first killed a person when he was eleven years old. He was forced to pull the trigger by the man who killed his father and mother. His anger has been with him so long he doesn't even remember his parents. Now he is a warlord in east Africa, a position of power that enables him to secure all the food he needs. Yesterday, he murdered two children who stole bread from him.

Cynthia has always done the right thing; even when her sister went "wild," she remained faithfully obedient to her parents. She made straight A's, married an accountant, and makes responsible decisions. She has never stolen, had more than one glass of wine, or cheated on her taxes. She is as perfect as you can imagine. Cynthia thought she had earned a healthy family, marriage, and life by doing everything right, but her husband rarely talks to her, her parents disapprove of her choice in wallpaper, and her four-year-old son doesn't obey.

Jared is homeless, Tobias has AIDS, Karen has never heard anyone say: "I am proud of you." Jorge is orphaned, Sonia is starving, Grandma Jean is lonely. On and on the stories go. This present life does not resemble the garden God created with Adam. It is the result of human brokenness — broken relationships that left the garden in exile and the broken culture that ensued.

Is this our future? Is there any hope for humanity? The only way to recover what has been lost is to return to God, to live in a restored relationship with him. There is one problem, however. The distrust and pride of humanity, what the Bible calls sin, ruins our relationship with God and damages our relationships with others. It's not that life is better with God, something we add on to what we have. It's that without God, we don't have true life at all. Lacking this restored relationship with God, we cannot truly live. The abundant life and purpose of Adam are lost to us as we live in our death and sin. Apart from God, we have no hope for the future. No purpose.

Fall from Perfect Relationship Continued: Abraham

The next major character in the narrative of the Bible is a man named Abraham. Following the fall of Adam and Eve, we learn from Genesis 3 through 11 that things go from bad to worse—murder, rape, and exploitation. In response to this, God selects a new "Adam" named Abraham. Seeking to redeem the damage done by Adam, God reissues a blessing and a command to Abraham:

> Now the LORD said to Abram, "Go from your country and your kindred and your father's house to the land that I will show you. And I will make of you a great nation, and I will bless you and make your name great, so that you will be a blessing. I will bless those who bless you, and him who dishonors you I will curse, and in you all the families of the earth shall be blessed." (Genesis 12:1–3)

With this blessing, God promises to make a lot of babies from Abraham (as many as the sand of the seashore, Genesis 22:17) and to create a new culture, the nation of Israel. The command and blessing of Adam are restated, but with a twist. This time, God will recreate the world from the inside-out. God's blessing will work outward from a single family to the world. God selects this new "Adam" and sends him to a new "garden" (Canaan), where he will make a new humanity to be a blessing to the entire world. Through this family, which grows into the people of Israel, the entire world will be blessed in the same way God had promised his blessing to Adam. Now, through Abraham, God will give abundant life and purpose to the world.

The hope for the future of the world that was once set on Adam is now laid on Abraham and his family. Abraham is not without failures, but he obeys God's command (to go to Canaan) and trusts God's promise (to receive a child). He passes the responsibility of being a blessing down his family line.

Life and Purpose for Israel

The descendants of Abraham, God's chosen instrument of blessing to the world, were to reflect the image and character of God to the rest of humanity. As God's people, the Israelites were to show the world what God is like by living in close relationship with him (Exodus 19:4–6) and imitating him. The rest of the world would be blessed by seeing the radical trust and obedience of Israel in the one, true God. Through Israel, the world could have a restored relationship with God.

With each passing generation, God provided for their needs, won battles for his people, protected them, and even spoke to them. God demonstrated to Abraham's descendants, over and over again, that he was loving, compassionate, and merciful. In a close relationship with him, they had abundant life. By obediently loving God, they would fulfill their divine purpose.

The Failure of Israel: Misplaced Hope and Trust

Sadly, like Adam, Israel failed to do what God had asked of them. Instead of pointing the world to God through obedience and love for him, they chose to follow the other nations and worship their false gods. They placed their hope and trust in idols made by human hands. From their top leaders to everyday farmers, Israel joined hands with the world in misplaced hope and trust. They rejected the honor of being God's family and chose to live on their own instead.

Their infidelity and rebellion wasn't confined to temples, but showed up in the way they treated one another. Called to be a nation that cared for the oppressed, they chose to exploit the vulnerable. Called to put themselves under God's rule and listen to his prophets, they chose to ignore the prophets' words and reject God's purpose.

For hundreds of years, Israel experienced cycles of *repentance* (re-trusting God) and *rebellion* (disobedience in the same old ways). Eventually, like Adam, they were exiled from the land they had been given. The history of Israel is a retelling of the history of Adam: sin-exile-reboot.

The story of God and his people, at this point, is one of lost hope and despair. The people who were supposed to bring blessing and life to the world instead brought more sin and death. The people of Israel couldn't even keep their own nation in order, much less be a blessing to the world. The hope that was hung on Israel's trust and obedience came crashing down as they turned to idols and rejected God.

Reverberations of Israel's Failure

What do we learn from these early scenes in the story? We see that humanity seems prone to settle for less. We repeatedly choose pleasure over lifelong relationships, comfort over lasting impact, cheap clothes over justice. Many people approach Christianity this way as well. Instead of grabbing onto the life Jesus offers, a life of joy filled with risk, they settle for an hour on Sunday or yearly attendance on Easter. This is the way of Adam and Israel. If you insist on making God's story all about you, it will lead you to the same place it led Adam and Israel—exiled from God and his garden. However, if you decide to make your story revolve around Christ, he will welcome you into the garden forever.

THE SUCCESS OF JESUS: MORE THAN REDEMPTION

We now come to the third major character in God's story: God's Son, Jesus Christ. Jesus gets some early press in the Old Testament when the prophets write about his coming as a king who will restore and renew the entire world.[19] The writers of the New Testament pick up this thread of sin-exile-reboot in the characters of Adam and Israel and show us that Jesus is yet another iteration of Adam and Israel. Paul writes: "Therefore, just as sin came into the world through one man, and death through sin, and so death spread to all men because all sinned … death reigned from Adam to Moses, even over those whose sinning was not like the transgression of Adam, who was a type of the one who was to come" (Romans 5:12–14).

Paul tells us that Adam was a *type* or a *shadow* of "the one who was to come," the true Adam. This means that in Adam we see a picture, a hint of what God had planned for the future. The true Adam, Jesus, is also an Israelite. As the story continues to unfold, we see the hope of the world shifting off Adam and Israel, who failed to carry the burden, and onto the back of Jesus. But what hope do we have with him bearing the burden? Why shouldn't he fail, just as the others did? Can he possibly undo the sadness and injustice, the sin and the exile of humanity? Will he be able to stop the cycle and start something new? The hope of the world hangs on this Second Adam, this true Israelite. Will he fail as Adam and Israel did, or will he succeed?

As we read the story of Jesus' life in the gospel of the New Testament, we learn that he was *radically* obedient to God. He loved his enemies, served the helpless, taught God's word, and kept God's commands even as he suffered rejection, scorn, trial, imprisonment, scourging, mockery, torture, and bloody crucifixion. He was a blessing to all who knew him, even extending his blessing to those who conspired to kill him. He died a martyr's death.

Jesus is certainly admirable. His life is a story of profound love. In fact, he was the one who coined the statement: "Greater love has no one than this, that someone lay down his life for his friends" (John 15:13). Jesus loved his friends, and he loved the world. And he died for those he loved. But he was not the only one who suffered death by crucifixion. In 4 BC, years before Jesus died on a cross, Roman general Varus crucified two thousand Jews (Josephus, *Ant.* 17.10). What, then, makes the death of this Jew any different from all the other martyrs of history?

The Bible reveals to us that the death of Christ was no ordinary martyrdom. His death was uniquely designed to break the cycle. No matter how many sin-exile-reboot cycles occurred, the flaw was in the system — in broken human DNA, our bentness away from God. What humanity needs is for God to enter the system, to redeem and renew the world from the inside out. No ordinary man could do this. Jesus, as the Son of God, redeems humanity, and eventually creation, through his death and resurrection.

Many have laid down their lives for those they love. I'm sure you have heard or read stories of sacrificial love. There is the story of a camp counselor who loses her life to save the life of a drowning child. Or a soldier who takes a bullet for his fellow combatant. We've heard about the mother who gives all her food to her starving child, only to lose her own life. Or the story of a friend who assumes the guilt and punishment of a crime for the person who is truly guilty.

Some of our most treasured stories tap into this kind of sacrificial love. Victor Hugo's Éponine dies to save Marius, Charles Dickens' Sydney Carton dies in Charles Darney's place, Harriet Stowe's Uncle Tom dies for Cassy and Emmeline, J. K. Rowling's Lily Potter dies to save Harry ... and there are others.

These stories of sacrifice for the sake of another all find their true meaning in the life of Jesus. Jesus laid down his life that others might live. Many of the great stories in Western literature echo this theme. However, Jesus' death was intended to break the *power* of death and give us life—to bring the dead back to life.

The Scope of Redemption

The scope of Jesus' death sets him apart from any other martyr. Jesus' sacrifice was not for a few, as we see in the stories just mentioned, but for many. The sacrificial benefit of his death crosses ethnic, cultural, and even temporal lines. In Christ, we see a selfless death on behalf of *all humanity*. Jesus is also different because, unlike the rest of us, he was the one, truly *obedient* man, the *faithful* Israelite who never disobeyed or abandoned God.

This cannot be said about any other person in history. In Jesus, we meet the true Adam, the faithful Israelite who dies to bear our sin and suffer our exile. We receive the benefits of his death on our behalf when we shift our trust from self to Jesus. He becomes our Savior, removing our guilt before God and extending us an offer of forgiveness. We no longer have to bear the punishment of death—exile from life with God—because Jesus suffers that for us.

All of this is admirable, even inspiring—but forgiveness of sin and escape from death alone are not enough to secure our transformation. A loving martyr in a grave, while inspiring, cannot change the world.

The Scope of Jesus' Resurrection

The striking point about Jesus' obedience, what makes his death so different, is that *he was obedient not only to the point of death but also to the point of life.* Jesus died to defeat sin, yes, but he rose to defeat death (Romans 5:15–21). Jesus' crucifixion sets him apart from all of the other martyrs of history *because he did not remain dead.* The grave could not contain him.

We should not even call Jesus a martyr; rather, he's the death-defeater. The first Adam brought death by disobedience, but through the second Adam came life! In 1 Corinthians 15:22, Paul writes: *"For as in Adam all die, so also in Christ shall all be made alive"* (italics added). All who put faith in Christ are made alive through the same power that raised him from the dead.

Through his obedience Jesus has changed the world—from the inside out. Instead of judging us from a distant cloud, he enters our world to bring life out of death, joy out of pain, hope out of despair. Jesus was obedient to God's purposes, not only to the point of death but also to the point of life. His death restores our relationship with God, and his resurrection ensures our eternal life. Jesus rolled back the failures of Abraham and his descendants by truly loving God, keeping all of God's commands. Jesus defeated the curse of Adam and restores and reunites humanity with God. But how?

Resurrection Life

What does his resurrection life resurrect?

First, it raises our *relationship with God* out of the grave. Deep, intimate relationship with God is restored in Christ.

Raised by the same Spirit that raised Jesus from the dead, we are ushered into God's new family to enjoy the love of the Father, Son, and Holy Spirit. Our humanity is brought back to life. Where we were once spiritually dead, we become spiritually alive, alert to the beauty, glory, and grace of God.

Second, our *purpose* is raised from the grave. Instead of living for ourselves, we can now live in joyful gratitude for God's grace, reflecting God's image by living in dependence on God's provision for us in Jesus. We get to be truly human again, fully alive as we pick up the creation mandate given to Adam, a mandate given a new twist through Jesus. Instead of making babies and making culture, we now make disciples and make culture in order to be a blessing to the world. The resurrection reunites us with God's plan to fill the world with his image (restored humanity), who create a kaleidoscope of cultures that showcase the glory of his grace.

To put it more plainly, the resurrection sends us back into relationships and the world with a mission of spreading God's grace to others. Contrary to some perceptions, Jesus didn't die and rise from the dead so we could attend religious services. Instead, Jesus was raised to be the first of a new humanity, a new creative work of God. As part of this work, we enjoy relationship with God and join him in his mission.

This is where your story can intersect with God's story. By putting your faith in Christ, you can receive new life and join God's redemptive agenda for the world. By faith in Jesus, we gain not just a better life but *true* life, life with

God, full of love and purpose. The resurrection changes everything — our self-understanding, our identity, our desires, our dreams. In the film *The Matrix*, the main character, Neo, is killed. His death is followed by a resurrection. Neo rises up after being shot to death by Agents, he twists his neck and flexes, and the entire Matrix bends around the power radiating from his new life. The vibrations of his resurrection visibly change the Matrix. The Operator watching can't make sense of it because the code's gone crazy.

Resurrection life is like that. It looks crazy, it bends the rules of this world, and it frees us to live as new people — not for ourselves, pursuing what we want, but lives of radical sacrifice, heartfelt generosity, genuine love, kindness, humility, and a sense of mission and purpose. When we receive this new life, we begin to live it out as new people who live in joyful obedience to their Savior.

If you have not received this blessing, we encourage you to stop trying to make a life for yourself and begin asking God to give you the life he has made for you in Christ. This exchange of your life for God's life, from your way of living to God's way of living, is called *repentance*. We make this exchange by faith, a lifestyle of dependence and trust in Jesus. We will unpack more of what this looks like in the next chapter.

If you are already a Christian and you are reading this, I would encourage you to press into the story of redemption. God has redeemed us from the failures of Adam and Israel and has raised us from death to be a new humanity, the people of God, a community called the Church. If you are part of this new humanity, your life will reflect it. People will sense the resurrection in your life. You will be a person who loves others and blesses the world. Can people sense these vibrations of resurrection life in you? Do they see "proof" that Jesus has risen from the dead in your life? In the resurrected Christ, we encounter a whole new way of being in the world—all things are made new.

The Reverberations of Jesus

All of this sounds pretty great, right? But what exactly do these "resurrection vibrations" look like? Let's circle back to look at some of those broken stories we mentioned earlier and see how Christ's resurrection can suffuse them with new life.

Bob now lives knowing that he is *accepted* by God. He is using his gifts and finances to help repair a broken world. He sold some of his homes and started a business that empowers locals throughout Africa to build and repair water wells. It was scary, but he sought forgiveness and restored relationship with his former wives and children. He lives an adventurous life, trusting in God and obeying his commands. He spends most of his evenings in his Manhattan flat, marveling at God's love for him and his newly formed relationship. Bob is at peace.

Sheryl is now *adopted* into the family of God. She is in a community of messed-up people who, like her, are learning to trust and obey Jesus. They care for one another. She still doesn't have much in terms of possessions. She also struggles to forgive her relatives that abused her. She is living without shame and without blame. She lives confidently knowing God loves her.

Togo weeps at the *forgiveness* of Jesus. He has confronted the wrongs he has done and is facing the consequences in the international court. He faces life in prison. He knows that this is not justice and that he deserves far worse punishment for the crimes he has committed. Because of this, he can't stop telling people about the hope and mercy he has now found in Christ. Togo is not angry. The region he used to control with an iron fist is now experiencing peace.

Cynthia stopped trying to earn the *approval* of others. No longer is she religious and self-righteous. Instead, she is finding the time to engage the resurrected life of humble service and joy. She and her husband are foster parents, trying to care for as many orphans as they can. She extends grace to her four-year-old and listens to him. For the first time in a decade, Cynthia talks regularly with her rebellious sister. She doesn't care what her parents think about her wallpaper choices; she knows Jesus died and rose again for her.

There are many stories like this. But what about your story? How is it being reshaped — raised to new life — because of Jesus' resurrection? Have you given Jesus an opportunity to change the way you think, the way you see yourself, or even the way you see others?

Remember: the resurrection changes *everything*.

CHAPTER 3

Stepping into the Resurrection

If Christ has not been raised, your faith is futile and you are still in your sins.

— 1 Corinthians 15:17

Up to now we have looked at how the resurrection of Jesus is both intellectually plausible and part of a larger, compelling story. In this chapter, we want to look more closely at how to participate in his resurrection life as well as what we lose if we refuse to embrace the resurrected Christ.

To do this, we will lift one sentence out of Paul's great chapter on the resurrection, 1 Corinthians 15. This chapter, part of a larger letter Paul wrote to a first-century church, contains fifty-eight verses of careful reasoning on the meaning and importance of the resurrection. Verse 17 gets to the crux of the matter: "If Christ has not been raised, your faith is futile and you are still in your sins." Here Paul puts it all on the line. If Christ hasn't been raised, the Christian faith is fiction and we are stranded in the fall of humanity, trapped in our imperfections. In other words, there is no hope, no purpose, no plan for the future. This is all there is.

But if the resurrection is true, it means there is hope; there is purpose and a plan for the future. How do we get connected to that? In order to understand how we can "get into" the resurrection, let's look closely at three essential but often misunderstood words Paul uses in this text—faith, sin, and Christ. If we can grasp what these words mean, we will be one step closer to seeing what we lose and what we gain by believing—or not believing—in the resurrection.

WHAT IS FAITH?

I realize *faith* is a somewhat nebulous word. As a noun, it can function as a catchall term for religion and spirituality. "What's your faith?" someone might ask, and the answers can fall anywhere on a spectrum from Scientology to Islam. Interfaith dialog is popular today. Unless you're an atheist with an ax to grind, having a "faith" is generally accepted. In some sectors of the U.S, it is becoming less cool to claim a religion, but that doesn't mean people lack faith.

Faith is also a verb. It is something you do. "Have faith," a person will say. We can wonder, "Faith in what?" In asking this, we tacitly recognize that faith is not just a religion—it is an action. Faith is an *activity* we all participate in. When we accept a job, we take it by faith. You can research the company, investigate their reputation, ask all the right questions, and come to the conclusion that this would be a great company to work for. You can get to the point where you believe this job is going to be a great fit, but you can't know it with 100 percent assurance. You can't be entirely confident that it will all work out. So when you accept the offer, you are accepting it on faith. You *believe* in the company, so to speak.

We do the same thing when we pick a spouse to marry. You can learn as much as you can about a boyfriend or girlfriend, date them for a while, observe their habits, make conclusions about their character and suitability, and then make a decision to marry them. You do this, believing that person will be a good life partner, but you don't *know* for certain until you act on your belief, until you step out on faith and say, "I do."

Everyone has faith. And everyone also doubts.

In his observations of pluralistic societies, Lesslie Newbigin noted that "doubt is not an autonomous activity."[20] What he means is that doubt is not self-sufficient — it cannot exist on its own. Doubt does not live in a vacuum. It is propped up by faith in something else. To doubt one thing is to have faith in another. Returning to our earlier example, if you put your faith in one company or spouse, you are — at the same time — expressing doubt in other companies or potential spouses. You are doubtful they are the best possible fit, uncertain they are the one for you. Meanwhile, you have faith in the other company or spouse. To put it another way, if you doubt one thing, it's because you believe in another.

With this in mind, let's apply this understanding of faith to the resurrection of Jesus.

If you doubt that a supernatural resurrection is possible, as many do, it's because you have faith in the possibilities that exist elsewhere. Perhaps you are trusting in the explanations of natural science. Many people in the West are prone to believe that only natural explanations can account for our world. This pervasive doubt in the possibility of the supernatural shows us where our faith actually lies—in the natural.[21] Our faith is in science.

Those who place their faith in science rely on it to settle questions of truth, meaning, and ultimate purpose. So the "religious" person isn't the only one who possesses faith. The secular person who trusts in science has faith too. One person believes that Jesus did rise from the dead; the other *believes* that Jesus didn't rise from the dead. But both of these beliefs are based on faith.

In this sense, even an atheist exercises faith. An atheist doubts God's existence while putting his faith in God's nonexistence. He cannot prove beyond a shadow of doubt that God does not exist. Everyone believes something, so faith puts everyone on the same playing field. We all start off with faith, even those of us who doubt. If this is true, it reframes the questions we have been asking about the resurrection. If we all have faith in something or someone, the real question isn't, "Should I believe or not believe?" but rather, "Is my belief well placed? Is it futile or fruitful?"

The word *faith*, though broadly used, can sometimes bring to mind negative connotations, things like irrational religion, wishful thinking, or even blind belief. Paul has none of these meanings in mind when he wrote: "And if Christ has not been raised, your faith is futile" (1 Corinthians 15:17). What does he mean when he says our faith is *futile* apart from the historic resurrection? The word *futile* actually means "fruitless." A fruitless faith is of little benefit. It is the result of putting your faith in something that isn't trustworthy. If the object of your faith can't stand up to your expectations, then it's useless to put your faith in it.

For instance, you might put momentary faith in a new restaurant or bottle of wine in order to experience some short-lived joy, only to taste its "fruits" and be disappointed. The restaurant or winery failed to stand up to your expectations. Your faith in the chef or vintner was misplaced. It was fruitless. Your faith was misdirected. That's essentially what Paul is saying here — if God did not, truly, raise Jesus from the dead, then Christian faith is fruitless. It is misdirected, misplaced.

Think about that for a moment. Don't rush past this. Paul, one of the key leaders of the Christian church, the writer of much of the New Testament, is telling us that Christian faith, minus the resurrection, is futile. A waste of time.

That seems a bit extreme, doesn't it? After all, Jesus lived an exemplary life, taught ideas that have influenced cultures all over the world, and even claimed to have suffered a substitutionary death for humanity. Even if you disagree with the purpose of his death, his martyrdom is certainly admirable. Shouldn't we celebrate Jesus' great teachings and his well-lived life? Aren't those of value? Calling the Christian faith (as a noun) fruitless does seem harsh. But this is not what Paul is saying. He is talking about faith (as a verb) expressed in Jesus. He's boiling his own Christianity down to the core and saying that if Jesus didn't rise from the dead, *then he's not worth trusting.*

This is particularly striking since Paul elsewhere wrote that he preached nothing but "Christ and him crucified" (1 Corinthians 2:2). So Paul tells us that when he preaches, he definitely talks about Jesus and his death (crucifixion). Isn't that the key message we need to share? That Jesus died and we can be forgiven? Isn't that the core; isn't that enough? But here Paul insists that the cross is *not* enough. This is because, for Paul and biblical Christianity, the cross doesn't exist apart from the resurrection. Good Friday needs the twin sister of Empty Tomb Sunday to be good; the cross requires the resurrection for faith in Christ to be fruitful.

In his letter to the Corinthians, Paul clearly connects removal of guilt with Jesus' death—but also with his return (1 Corinthians 1:8). This tells us that there is an unbreakable link between Jesus' death and his resurrection. If Jesus did *not* rise from the dead, then he *cannot* exercise victory over sin, death, or evil. He *cannot* maintain our innocence before God, impart us new life through the Spirit, or return to make the world new — all things that Jesus said he would do. Without the resurrection, Jesus' teachings are a sham, half-baked ideas from a wandering Jew with a messiah complex. But with the resurrection, his teachings and actions have power to overturn sin, death, and evil and create a whole new humanity.

This is not a life-and-death matter; it is a matter of death *for* life. Jesus does not claim to die — period. He claims to have died *and risen to life.* This means that if we have faith in Jesus as a moral philosopher, a good example, or even a suffering savior, it is not enough. *Biblical faith is faith in a resurrected Christ.* Paul is saying that in order for our faith to be fruitful and real, it has to be based on the power of a new life.

We'll come back to this a bit later when we consider Christ, but for now, we need to recognize two main things about faith. First, we all have faith. Second, the object of our faith needs to live up to our expectations, and Jesus' expectations for you are nothing short of a new life. Jesus Christ isn't just asking you to believe he existed and that he died. He is asking for your faith, for you to put all your expectations, hopes, dreams, desires, wants, and needs on him. He is asking you to trust him over companies, spouses, chefs, and vintners. Biblical faith is thoughtful trust in the good news that Jesus has succeeded where Adam failed, that he alone has the power to reverse the curse, forgive sin, conquer death, and give us new life. If we put our faith in the wrong thing, even a crucified, non-resurrected messiah, we are still in our sins.

This brings us to the second word we need to understand — *sin*.

WHAT IS SIN?

Sin is a deeply misunderstood word. When people hear "sins," they often hear "rules." Some people like to break the rules; others like to keep them. Yet both the rule-breaking secularist and the rule-keeping religious person miss the real meaning of sin. What makes sin a sin? It isn't just that we break a holy rule. You might say there is a sin underneath the sin. Underneath our behavioral issues, we have trust issues. Sin surfaces when deep down we choose to *trust in some thing more than we trust in God*.

When we trust in something more than God, we are saying that that thing is more trustworthy — more worthy of our faith than God. In that moment of sin, we believe that our object of trust is more reliable and more deserving of our devotion than God. That thing is made into a functional god, what the Bible calls an *idol*.

So what does this look like in real life? Let's consider a sin like pride. Pride isn't a sin just because society tends to look down on it (note that some forms of pride are rewarded). Nor is pride a sin simply because God says it's a sin (he does, of course, oppose the proud and shows grace to the humble). Pride is sinful because it involves putting our ultimate trust in ourselves rather than God. The proud person, certain she is right, lifts herself up, exalting herself over others to find her worth and value. She insists that others recognize that *she is correct.* The proud person will insist on being right, even when she is wrong.

So while we see pride on the surface, underneath that proud display is the idolatry of *self.* The proud make a god out of themselves and being right (or great) instead of marveling at God's rightness and greatness. This is why God is opposed to the proud, because they have set themselves up as a rival god. Both secular and religious people commit the "sin" of pride. Or to say it another way: sin is placing your faith in something other than God, and the proud person places faith in himself or herself.

"Secular" Sin

In the human search for meaning and life, our desires tend to run in one of two directions—*secular* or *religious.* Secular people remove themselves from the supernatural story to find meaning and life on their own, in what they can understand and experience. I followed this path for many years. At age nineteen, I went away to college and met a young cheerleader and fell in love (or so I thought). We dated, slept together, and stole out of our dorm rooms to be together. I'd scrape money together, even if I had to break the bank, just to get a hotel room with her for the night. It wasn't love — it was lust, the pursuit of pleasure for myself.

One night, she called me and was in tears. We met in the dorm lobby and she choked out her pain. Her father had left an angry, cursing message on her voicemail machine. He was upset, and he was coming to school to get her and take her home. Worst of all, she confided in me that she had been abused by her father growing up. He had peeked in on her while she was showering, had emotionally and verbally abused her, and more. What was I to do? I called my parents and shared the situation. Then, without telling them, I did what I thought was right in that moment. I decided I would come to her rescue by marrying her. That's right. We eloped.

We were wed by a Justice of the Peace in a shifty county legal office in Tyler, Texas. Excited that I had done the right thing, I called my parents to announce the good news. I knew they would be so proud of me. I dialed my parents' number on a pay phone and my mother picked up. As I began sharing, I'll never forget the shrill cry of her voice on the other end of the phone. She was devastated. Angry, I told her she should be proud of me and that I loved this girl. Before hanging up, my mom said to me: "Jonathan, she's not telling you everything." Those words echoed in my mind over the next couple days. Clearly things hadn't gone as I had planned or hoped they would, so we went home to make things right with our parents. Over the next week, I discovered that my new wife had lied — about *everything*.

I soon learned that she had made up the entire story. She *was* getting kicked out of school, but it was for having bad grades. Why had she lied about her father abusing her? Because she had known that I would come to her rescue, and if I did, she would get to keep me. She had lied all the way to the altar to keep me as her boyfriend and now as her husband. I was bewildered. Lost. I felt like someone had leveled a shotgun at my heart and blown it into a thousand pieces. The Texas court issued a rare annulment of the marriage based on fraud, but nothing could annul the pain I felt.

For years after this, I self-medicated with several women and various relationships, trying to numb the pain in relationship after relationship. Looking back, I now see that my hunger for these relationships sprang from an inordinate desire to be deeply loved by a woman, to know intimate affection and relational intimacy. I lived a *secular* life, living without looking to God for the things I wanted: affection, intimacy, and love. When I thought about God, I often felt guilt and shame.

At one point, I went off to a Bible School in the rolling green hills of the English Lake District to get things right with God, but I found another lover instead. At night, I would sneak out to be with her and to go drinking in the pubs. Eventually, we were found out and I was kicked out of Bible School, the very school where my parents had met twenty years earlier. I made yet another call to my parents, this time well aware of my shame.

Why do I share this story? To show what it is like to live a secular life, putting your faith in the world to meet your needs. A religious person would say that my lustful pursuits weren't a matter of faith — they were a sign of my rebellion. My sin? Having sex before marriage. And to be sure, I broke that rule, but my sin ran deeper than that. My faith was in intimacy and feminine affection, that they would somehow meet my longings, my needs. I was trying to make up for the deceitful affection and the pain of a broken relationship. My sin was putting faith in women, instead of God. I was looking for an extraordinary thing (deep, never-ending intimacy) in a lovely but ordinary thing (women). There was temporary joy, but not the deep and enduring love, meaning, and intimacy provided uniquely for me in Jesus Christ. My trust in the pleasures of the secular world was fruitless.

"Religious" Sin

I've also walked the religious path of faith. I had a genuine encounter with the risen Christ when I was six years old. I was taken by the notion that the God of the universe wanted me to be his son, to bring me into his family and receive his perfect love. I knew God wasn't offering me this privilege because I had accomplished anything — I was only six — but, rather, because he had accomplished so much for me in Christ. Jesus was the proof of his love for me.

As I grew older, I slowly took my eyes off of Jesus and lost my childlike faith. Instead of trusting in Christ, I began to trust in myself. I continually felt as if I needed to do something to get back on God's good side. I knew that I had blown it as a professional Christian — premarital sex, divorce/annulment, getting kicked out of Bible school — but I still wanted to set things straight, to make up for my past, to make God proud. So I committed myself to rigorous Bible study and extended times of prayer and fasting, and I asked God to "break me" over and over again because of my sin. I sought out accountability relationships where I asked people to interrogate my holiness. They asked me questions like: Did you look at pornography? Did you have a devotional time each day? Did you handle your finances well? And at the end, did you lie on any of the above?

A lot of these ordinary virtues became extraordinary in my own eyes. If I kept the list, I was high. If I broke the rules, I was low. I had taken God out of the center of my faith and replaced him with rules. How well I kept these rules helped me gauge my performance. Sometimes I would break the rules, lack affection for God, fall back into lust, and prove ineffective in sharing my faith. My faith was futile — it was focused entirely on myself.

Instead of trusting in reason, experience, and the pleasures of this world, the religious person trusts in religious activity for meaning and life. Like secularism, this can be diverse, taking on all kinds of different forms depending on the religion of choice. In aberrant forms of Christianity, meaning and acceptance are found in doing various spiritual disciplines, having good church attendance, following certain rules (at least visibly), and following certain methods to share your faith regularly.

So as a religious person, what was the sin beneath my sin? It was my own self-righteousness. My desire was to be right, good, and holy enough for God *without* God's help. Like the secular person, I had excluded God. Instead of looking to the world for meaning and comfort, I was proudly insisting that I could make my own way to God. My superficial view of sin led me to put faith in my rule-keeping ability, not in Christ, who had kept all the rules for me. My faith was in what I could do for God, not in what he had done for me.

As a result, I was full of religious sin, self-righteous attempts to improve on what God offered to me in Jesus. My sin was self-righteousness, and beneath that sin lurked the god of self. I had put my faith in my religious performance. Yes, even the religious person can have misdirected faith.

If both the secular and the religious person misplace their faith (sin), is there another way? This brings us to Christ.

WHO IS CHRIST?

Recall where we began. Paul wrote that if Christ has not been raised, then our faith is futile and we are still in our sins. How, then, does faith in a resurrected Christ rescue us from this futility? How does the resurrection remedy the misplaced faith of secular *and* religious sin?

Let's think about this in three ways.

First, Jesus' resurrection implies his death, which forgives us for the cosmic crime of treasonous faith in other things. We have all betrayed God by trusting the fleeting promises of the world or our own religious performance. Simply put, we all cherish things, people, and objects more than God. Coming to grips with this would be dismal, a reason for hopeless despair, were it not for the hope of the cross. Through the cross Jesus obtains forgiveness for our sins: "In him [Christ] we have redemption through his blood [the cross], the forgiveness of our sins, in accordance with the riches of God's grace" (Ephesians 1:7 NIV).

This is a marvelous truth. Jesus alleviates our treasonous guilt by bearing our onerous sentence—the curse of death. The crucifixion tells us that our rightful guilt is relieved by his wrongful death in order to grant us a grace-filled life. At the cross, Jesus mercifully bears the punishment for our crime. The resurrection points us back to the cross, where we receive profound mercy. This should floor us. Such an undeserved act, shown by a God deserving of our every devotion, reveals the depth of his devotion to us as his Son suffers and writhes in our place. This is not only mercy (not getting what we deserve); it is grace (getting more than we deserve).

The cross is not just about sinners avoiding punishment—it is about God showing us love. The resurrection reminds us of the mercy and grace that is bound up in the cross, grace that has the power to change a person through and through, even if that change is a gradual process. Receiving this divine mercy that forgives your sins and transforms your life is your first step into the resurrection.

The second reason Jesus is the right place for our faith is because he is "the resurrection and the life" (John 11:25). It is important that we grasp that believing in Jesus is not just faith "in the resurrection" as a supernatural, historical event; it is faith in a resurrected Christ, a person. Here is why faith in the resurrected Christ makes all the difference. Jesus' resurrection demonstrates his power over death, which proves that he uniquely has *the power of life.*

By rising from the dead, Jesus is saying to both the secular and the religious person: "In your search for meaning, worth, acceptance, and love, I'm what you've been looking for. I alone can give you life. All the greatness, acceptance, beauty, and love you desire is found in me. Your God-sized desire for intimacy is meant to be fulfilled in the God of life. Faith in ordinary things can't give you that. That's futile faith because it demands the extraordinary from the ordinary. Futile faith can't give life. But a God-sized person who defeats death has all the power to give you what you are looking for. I can fulfill your heart's desires."

When we put our faith in a resurrected Christ, we redirect all our desires back to their origin. Like tracing divine threads of joy, meaning, and purpose all the way back to the source, the door of desire swings wide open and there stands a resurrected, radiant Jesus, full of never-waning life. Jesus isn't standing there with his finger wagging, scolding us for our desire to be loved, accepted, and beautiful. He's showing us that he, together with his Father and the Spirit, is where we find true love, acceptance, beauty, and greatness. The resurrection shows us that Jesus alone can give us life because he *is* the life: "In him was life, and the life was the light of men" (John 1:4). Receiving this tremendous, radiant life is how you step into the resurrection.

Third, the resurrection tells us that Jesus can satisfy our God-sized desires not only in this life, but also in life after death. Those who put their faith in Christ are promised a resurrection body like his to enjoy his love, acceptance, meaning, beauty, and greatness forever. If Christ has not been raised, we are not only stuck in a tailspin of desire in this life, but we are denied finding fulfillment in the life to come. However, if Christ has been raised, we will forever have fulfillment of our desire and the final target for our faith.

There is no greater step into enlightenment than Jesus; he is "the light of the knowledge of the glory of God" (2 Corinthians 4:6). The resurrection tells us where to find never-ending life and joy—in the resurrected Christ. Faith in Jesus will bear fruit not just in this life but also in the life to come. Receiving this promise of bodily resurrection life will be our final step into the resurrection. If Christ has not been raised, we remain in our sins and our faith is futile. But Christ has been raised; therefore, your faith in him will be forever fruitful.

With faith, sin, and Christ cleared up a bit, what do you think? With the plausibility of the resurrection established in chapter 1, the narrative appeal of how the resurrection changes history in chapter 2, and now, a sense of why we all need a resurrected Messiah in chapter 3 — do you see where your faith may be misplaced? Do you see that sin is deeper than morality, that it distorts our sense of where true meaning, joy, and purpose come from?

Jesus wants to rescue us from this and restore us into true joy, profound meaning, and eternal purpose. If you want this, acknowledging it to God and exchanging your misplaced faith for faith in the risen Jesus will bring you into his saving grace. If you still doubt, we want to grant you the dignity of your own beliefs and leave plenty of space to wrestle through doubts, but we hope that we've helped you do that with greater integrity and clarity. Wherever you are, stick with us through the final chapter to see the benefits of the resurrected life.

CHAPTER 4

How the Resurrection Changes Everything

"And behold, I am with you always, to the end of the age."

—Matthew 28:20

In just a short time we have made our way through doubts, a cosmic story of redemption, and a new understanding of what it means to have faith. We've talked about what it means to doubt the resurrection, we've noted how the resurrection fits into the larger story of God, and we've seen how the resurrection is a thunderclap affirming the life-giving power that Jesus has to forgive *and* transform our lives today. But what does it mean, practically, to live in light of the resurrection? What difference does Jesus' resurrection make in the lives of those who believe?

Whether you are someone who doubts and struggles to believe that a Jewish man beat death, or someone who attends Easter services every year, it is worth your time to consider what belief in Jesus *produces*. In other words, how does the death and resurrection of Jesus change a life? What does that look like?

As you can imagine, moving from doubt and into belief promises to radically reorient your life, your goals, and your dreams. In a real sense, it is like shifting from death to life. In this chapter we'll explore how the story of Easter will change your life.

There is no better place to look for these answers than Jesus himself. Our understanding of the resurrected life begins with him and his words. Jesus claims that his resurrection establishes a new *authority*, new *identity*, and new *mission*. After unpacking what this means, we will look at the daily lives of people who have walked from doubt to belief in resurrection. Their lives and stories give evidence that Jesus' claims lead to new life.

BENEFITS: NEW AUTHORITY, IDENTITY, MISSION

The last lines of Matthew's Gospel belong to Jesus. Believers in the resurrection cherish them because they are the final words of their Savior. In his words Jesus explains how to live the resurrected life and speaks of the benefits that faith produces. He tells his disciples how to be fruitful and multiply with their new, abundant life. He describes a life characterized by a new authority, a new identity, and a new mission:

Now the eleven disciples went to Galilee, to the mountain where Jesus had directed them. And when they saw him they worshiped him, but some doubted. And Jesus came to them and said, "All authority in heaven and on earth has been given to me. Go therefore and make disciples of all nations, baptizing them in the name of the Father and of the Son and of the Holy Spirit, teaching them to observe all that I have commanded you. And behold, I am with you always, to the end of the age." (Matthew 28:16–20)

A New Authority: Follow Me

Jesus begins with his place in the world, making a claim of authority. As the one who has laid down his life for the world and defeated death, Jesus now claims to have all authority in heaven and on earth. This claim of authority eclipses that of kings or the leaders of nations. Other kings die, but Jesus vanquished death. Rulers are made, but Jesus is the one who made all things. His rule extends beyond the earth into the heavens, where he deposes powers and brings all who are in opposition to surrender, establishing never-ending peace. Paul poetically describes his lordship:

[Jesus] is before all things, and in him all things hold together. And he is the head of the body, the church. He is the beginning, the firstborn from the dead, that in everything he might be preeminent. For in him all the fullness of God was pleased to dwell, and through him to reconcile to himself all things, whether on earth or in heaven, making peace by the blood of his cross. (Colossians 1:17–20)

The risen Jesus has all the authority in the universe, and he is profoundly great and good. He deserves our worship and obedience. Those who possess resurrected life joyfully acknowledge that Jesus is in charge and they follow him, listening to what he says and reading his teachings to line their lives up in obedience to his commands. A disciple learns to submit to Jesus in every facet of life. From waking up to going to bed, everything in life falls under his authority. Our short-term plans and long-term investments are informed by his instruction.

Living the resurrected life, then, means placing yourself under Christ's rule. He is in charge, and he is good at what he does. As you wrestle with your doubts about Jesus and the resurrection, know this: Jesus is no tyrant. He does not abuse his power. Rather, he is a loving and serving master. He is the master who washes his disciples' feet. He is the king who lays down his life for his friends — and, yes, even for those who doubt him. You will not be cheated. You can run the cost-benefit analysis of trusting Jesus a million times, but it always comes out the same. The cost of submitting to Jesus pales in comparison with the rich relationship and future you have in Christ.

There are four primary ways in which we can follow Jesus:

1. *In community.* Following Jesus isn't something we do in isolation — it's communal. You need others and they need you. As a community, we share in each other's struggles and daily remind one another of

the abundant life and the precious Savior we have in common. Christians gather on Sundays not only to sing to God, but also to each other: "Jesus rose from the dead!"

2. *In prayer.* Have you ever wondered *why* Christians pray? They pray because they know how dependent they are on God. Prayer is an invitation to depend on God, trusting him by joining his agenda for our lives.

3. *In repentance and faith.* Repentance and faith are integral to the Christian life. Repentance is more than feeling sorry so we get on God's good side. It is turning from the fleeting promises of sin to the superior promises of the Savior. It is seeing that, by grace, we are already on God's good side and nothing else can compare to him.

4. *In the story.* Despite its age and apparent obscurity, the Bible is the story and the inspired text of God. It teaches us how to follow Jesus. We read it not to learn about extinct cultures, but to know and follow our Savior who was raised.

New Identity: In Christ

Jesus, with complete authority, gives us a new source of identity. Resurrection life is nothing short of an entirely new identity. Early believers in resurrection went as far as to say they were new creatures. Their old definitions of themselves no longer applied as they began to understand who they were by Jesus' words to them. In American culture, we define ourselves by things like sexual orientation, political party, race, religion, or even our home state. You can find your identity in your occupation, your alma mater, your hobbies, and even your clothes. An easy way to locate where you find your identity is to fill in the blank to this "I am _____" statement. For example, someone could say:

- I am an accountant.
- I am a Buddhist.
- I am an alcoholic.
- I am a vegetarian.
- I am a Longhorn.
- I am a skater.
- I am white.
- I am a Democrat.
- I am gay.
- I am beautiful.
- I am a hipster.
- I am a disciple.
- I am a Christian.

Usually, our identity will emerge as a composite of the things listed. It will have a hidden mantra that goes something like this: I am what I eat, who I sleep with, how I make money, what I wear, what I look like, or where I came from. How we view ourselves is closely tied to how well we are doing in these various arenas of life. Yet some of these statements will have a stronger influence than others. How do you know which is strongest? Think about the ones that you just can't live without. If you cannot imagine yourself without that statement being true, you have likely found something that is core to your identity.

The interesting thing about all of these identities is that they depend on what we *do*. But the resurrected life is different. Instead of being named by the things we have done, we are named "in the Father, and of the Son, and of the Holy Spirit." We are no longer defined by our rise and fall in success and failure. Instead, our identity is defined by God's utter success over our sinful failures and his gift of new life. We have a new identity. The New Testament describes our newfound identity in these ways:

- Child of God
- Friend of God
- Servant
- Sent one
- Reconciler
- Disciple
- Blessed
- New Creation
- Saint or Holy One

This list only scratches the surface of our new identity in Christ. And this new identity is a gift of grace—we don't deserve it. Yet Christ's work is to give this to us. They are ways in which we understand who we are in light of what he has done for us, not what we have done for him. He is Father to the child, Friend to the friend, Master to the servant, Ultimate Missionary to the sent one, Savior to the disciple, Resurrection to the new creation, Holy to the saint.

Empowered by the Presence of God

Jesus' final words make it clear that we will not be abandoned: "And behold, I am with you always, to the end of the age." The resurrected Jesus is not in a distant universe, looking down from the clouds to see how well we are doing. He is with us and he will be with us forever. The resurrected life is a continually restored relationship with God. Unlike Adam or Israel, we will not be exiled. We will no longer be alone. Instead, we will be with God forever. This is the ultimate benefit of following Jesus: Jesus *himself*. We can daily enjoy relationship with him. Like Adam and Eve in the garden, we can walk with God in the midst of our day.

This promise of God's presence isn't a fleeting greeting we scribble on the inside of a Hallmark card. It is a true statement that brings us real comfort and power. As Jesus was preparing his disciples, he told them he would send them the Holy Spirit. In the Bible, the book of Acts tells the story of how the Holy Spirit empowers normal people to follow Jesus. We see the Spirit empowering ordinary people like you and me to speak the gospel boldly, obey Jesus' commands, heal the sick, make disciples, give generously, and care for the poor. The Holy Spirit is the divine person who possesses resurrection power and makes it available to us: "If the Spirit of him who raised Jesus from the dead dwells in you, he who raised Christ Jesus from the dead will also give life to your mortal bodies through his Spirit who dwells in you" (Romans 8:11). The power of the resurrection is ours, alive in us through the Spirit!

When we think about changing our lives, we can easily start by saying to ourselves: "Let's get to work ... I can do this!" But if you set off in your own resolve, you will fall flat. I do all the time. When I'm not living out of resurrection power (depending on the Spirit through prayer), I end up relying on my own emotional power. If I feel good today, I'll try my best to follow Jesus. If I don't feel that great, I'll struggle. Either way, I'm missing the vibrancy of the Spirit. I quickly tire out, snap at others, or silently take credit for the good things I do. I begin building up my own self-righteousness through self-dependence.

However, when I begin the day in utter dependence on the Spirit, drawing near to God in prayer and asking for his power and guidance throughout the day, it changes things entirely. Instead of tiring out, I'm filled up. Instead of snapping at others, I find a hesitating nudge from the Spirit to love and forbear. Instead of taking credit, I'm quick to give glory to God. The Holy Spirit enables you to live the resurrected life. He bears the fruit of love, joy, peace, patience, kindness, goodness, faithfulness, gentleness, and self-control, even in difficult circumstances. You don't have to muster up the strength to follow Jesus. Instead, you need to rely on the strength of the Holy Spirit.

New Mission: Make Disciples

Matthew 28:18–20 is what Christians call the Great Commission, the dominant marching orders for all who have faith in resurrection. It can sound a bit militant: "Take God's authority and make disciples." But remember, these orders are from the one who has laid down his life to save his enemies. Ironically, our orders are to invite through imitation. Our mission is to make disciples through our words *and* actions. Or, as Jesus said, "teach and obey." In fact, it is when we experience the riches of renewal through Christ that we become, as Eugene Peterson says, "God's advertisement to the world."[22] We make disciples by living resurrected lives and telling people about the resurrected Christ.

There's not a hint of coercion here. It's a life of love. Jesus wants us to spread the gospel throughout the world by spending our lives for the sake of others. The power of the resurrection doesn't *end* with us; it travels *through* us. Our commission is invitation. We invite others to join God's redemptive agenda to restore human flourishing and remake the world. We are sent into the world to share the good news that Jesus has defeated sin, death, and evil through his own death and resurrection. Jesus is making all things new, and he calls his followers to participate in his work of renewal.

Distinctive Discipleship

Part of what makes this command such a "great" mission is its scope — *all nations*. When Jesus spoke these words, he was reorienting a primarily Jewish audience to a distinctly multiethnic mission. The Greek word used here is the same word that gives us the English word "ethnic." It refers to the *nations*, not modernist geopolitical states, but non-Jewish people groups (Gentiles) with distinct cultures and languages. Our commission is not to Christianize nation-states, but to share the good news of what Jesus has done with all ethnic groups. Christ does not advocate what is commonly called Christendom, a top-down political Christianity. Instead, he calls his followers to transmit a bottom-up, indigenous Christianity, to all peoples *in all cultures*.

We should also note that this command is to make disciples *of* all nations, not *from* all nations. The goal of Christian missions is not to replace the rich diversity of human culture for a cheap consumer, Christian knock-off culture. Dr. Andrew Walls puts it well:

> Conversion to Christ does not produce a bland universal citizenship: it produces distinctive discipleship, as diverse and variegated as human life itself. Christ in redeeming humanity brings, by the process of discipleship, all the richness of humanity's infinitude of cultures and subcultures into the variegated splendor of the Full Grown Humanity to which the apostolic literature points (Eph 4.8 – 13).[23]

What we should strive for is *distinctive discipleship*, discipleship that uniquely expresses personal faith in our cultural context. Disciples in urban Manhattan will look different than disciples in rural Maehongson. These differences allow for a flourishing of the gospel that contributes to the many-splendored new humanity of Christ. Simply put, the message of Jesus is for the flourishing of all humanity in all cultures.

Jesus informs our resurrected life. He gives us a new and gracious authority, a new identity, and a new mission. With that in view, what does it look like to participate in this task of renewing the world? Where do we begin? Jesus has painted for us a great picture of the new life. Let's turn now to the *daily* implications of resurrection life.

IMPLICATIONS: RISKING FOR HUMANITY

If Jesus did, indeed, rise from the dead, we have nothing to fear and everything we need. All that we strive for is fulfilled in Jesus. All that we seek to avoid has been resolved by him. For example, if Jesus rose from the dead, we no longer need to strive for acceptance because we are now accepted by him. If Jesus rose from the dead, we don't need to fear death, because it has been defeated. This means that we are free to smuggle medical supplies into Burma, even at the risk of death, knowing that our eternal fate is already sealed. We can move to distant countries to invest in development and renewal because Christ did the same for the world. Like the early Christians, we can care for the poor and marginalized in our cities. If we have resurrection life, we will have courage to take risks in the name of love.

A close friend of mine is starting a coffee-roasting business with the aim of one day moving to Mumbai, India, to aid an organization that cares for children and women exploited in sex trafficking. It is wonderful and it is risky. He purchases beans from India, roasts them, and sells them to raise awareness. The profits go back into helping folks start a new resurrected life. My friend could lose everything in the business. He is leaving behind his extended family and the comforts of home. That's the power of the resurrection in our lives. The resurrected Jesus leads us and empowers us to use all of our gifts and all of our lives for the flourishing of others.

Risking our lives for the sake of others looks different for each person. It comes in all kinds of forms, from sacrifice to celebration. Let's close by looking at three implications of resurrection life: give, celebrate, and serve.

Give

Disciples of Jesus will no longer hoard what they have. Instead, they give it away. The hope of resurrection frees us to live generous lives. When we look at our hands, our bank accounts, our homes, and our time, we ask, "God, how can I be a blessing to your people?" There is no need to hoard possessions because you have abundant life in Jesus. You invest your life in his calling to make disciples. This is no overnight task; it's a lifetime endeavor.

Making disciples will bring you joy and hardship. After all, this invitation is radical — exchange your authority for Jesus' authority, your self-made identity for his better identity, your purpose for his purpose. But this is how the resurrection works: in dying to ourselves we receive the life Jesus offers. Every gift and "sacrifice" we make becomes another opportunity to realize the greatness and goodness of God's gift to us in the resurrected Christ.

What does this kind of giving look like in normal, everyday life? My wife makes the best cookies in the world. I didn't come to that conclusion on my own; it has been confirmed by people all over the world. I won't give away the recipe, but I will say that within each bite of cookie, you experience the pleasing combination of Nutella, dark chocolate chips, sea salt, and browned butter. Baking these cookies is a three-stage process that changes people's lives.

We live in a middle class neighborhood where everyone has everything they need. So blessing and giving for my wife looks like this: baking cookies on the dark and rainy days here in Portland and giving all of them away. As kids and adults arrive home after long days at school and work, they are met by warm cookies. While they are working hard throughout the day, she is working hard to bless them on their return. She gives up her day for the benefit of others. Our neighbors are overjoyed, thankful, and quite honestly, comforted. Who doesn't like coming home to homemade cookies? This is something simple, but it is an everyday picture of the resurrected life. We give abundantly from what we have to bless others.

Celebrate

Part of experiencing the power of the resurrected life is sensing your need to pause regularly and celebrate. You can sing, dance, paint, and bake all in praise of God's goodness. You can marvel at the story of God and the honor you have to participate in it. All are welcome at these celebrations: the shy, the awkward, and the rude. Our parties will be open and welcoming because we know that Christ came to us when we were not desirable and invited us to join him. Who Jesus is and what he has done is at the center of your joyful celebration.

We have one of these times of celebration every year on the Fourth of July. It's one of the high points in our community calendar. Our front yard becomes a big party space as neighbors, coworkers, and friends gather to celebrate on our front porch. The day is marked by good drink, good food, and good conversation for everyone (young and old). We start at lunch and go until dark, when we shoot off small firecrackers in the street with all the neighborhood kids.

The first year we did this was marked by an impromptu jam session. I found myself playing bass guitar on a neighbor's porch for four hours. Alongside me was a semi-retired artist, a realtor, a friend from out of town, and a chorus of folks dancing and cheering us on while little kids colored every inch of the sidewalk with chalk. Hopefully you have experienced a party like this in your lifetime. Maybe it was a wedding, Thanksgiving, or just a gathering of friends. If you have, you have tasted the sort of community and celebration that the resurrected life produces. Imagine a celebration not about independence from a European power, or birthdays, or even a new marriage, but a celebration of death defeated and life forever. That is a party. That is joy.

I live in a city where less than 4 percent of the population believes Jesus rose from the dead. Even fewer go to gatherings to celebrate Jesus. While most of the city is making brunch plans, our church is meeting in a dance venue. Musicians are crafting tunes as they invite everyone to participate in celebrating Jesus and the joy of the resurrected life. We listen to a teacher expound on the story of God, reminding us why we are here and what we are here to do. People shout, sing, dance, and smile. We hug one another and encourage each other to live courageous and generous lives of love. Why? Because Jesus rose from the dead. Isn't that reason to celebrate early on a Sunday morning? Who is welcome? Everyone!

Serve

If Christ has reconciled us to himself, serving us in our rebellion and sin, we should follow his example and seek reconciliation with others. Because Christ has served us, we are free to follow Jesus in caring for the vulnerable and those who need to hear the story of God.

Yes, it will be a struggle and a sacrifice. You will need to fight for reconciliation sometimes. Where there are disagreements, you will fight for peace. Where there is injustice, you will need to find creative ways to bring justice. Jesus did everything needed to restore the relationship between God and humanity, and you are now invited to join him in his work of restoring broken relationships.

This may take the form of adopting orphans or caring for teenage mothers. It could look like hosting the homeless and visiting prisoners. You will need to fight for justice and for people to be treated as people of worth and value, people for whom God's Son gave his life to save. You will daily need to ask yourself: "How can I bring hope and love into this world, this city, and my neighborhood?"

A couple named the Pauls are in their fifties. They live in inner-city Portland, a neighborhood that is a cocktail of the rich and poor. Historically, this had been a low-income area of the city, but it has now become a haven for the city's growing creative class. Some of them, like the Pauls, are Christians, and they intentionally moved there to make disciples. Almost instantly, this couple became grandparents to the neighborhood. They opened their home for art camps, garden clubs, and college football on Saturdays. They have invested relationally in the neighborhood — from the gas station employees to small business owners. They listen to people and welcome them into their lives. They are famous for serving and sharing God's love with everyone.

But what is remarkable to their neighbors is the Pauls'

story. The Pauls are from Arkansas, well on their way to a retirement lifestyle of babysitting their grandchildren. Then, they sensed God calling them to move to Portland. They had a comfortable, suburban home, but left that comfort to go to a culture and city completely foreign to their own. They arrived in the city as servants, dedicated to giving their lives away. If you ask them how it's going, if it has been worth the sacrifices, they will smile and say: "We can't imagine living any other way. We won't go back to the way things were before."

This is the power of the resurrected life. Serving others is a sacrifice, yes. But that sacrifice is filled with joy. You won't be able to imagine living any other way.

Why?

Jesus tells those who follow him to leave all they have behind, to give their lives to the poor, to love their enemies, and to be a blessing to the world. Let's not pretend this is easy to do. Following Jesus will require your whole life. Not just part of it. Not just your leisure time. Not just some of your budget. No, it requires your whole life. It will feel like death and suffering at times. It will feel that way because you are laying your life down. That's what the resurrection looks like in daily life. We do not hold anything back—our talents, possessions, or time—because we live with the certainty that death and sin have been defeated.

There is no sugarcoating it. You will lose your life. In its place you will find a vibrant, full, and eternal life. By dying to ourselves we become alive to the power of Christ through the Holy Spirit. The same power that raised Jesus from the dead empowers us to live a life for Jesus. His death and resurrection have become our death and resurrection. Our old life is gone, and we now experience a new authority, identity, and mission. This is why we give, celebrate, and serve: we have died and have been raised again to experience new and abundant life.

DREAM OF THE WORLD TO COME

In the world that is to come, we will roam a whole new creation, not as witless spirits or flittering angels, but as restored people in bodily glory. Like Jesus, we too will possess resurrected bodies: "But in fact Christ has been raised from the dead, the firstfruits of those who have fallen asleep" (1 Corinthians 15:20). Jesus is the first of the future harvest, the best of the crop of a whole new humanity. He is the perfected prototype of human glory. All who are in Christ will follow. Paul describes our new bodies as possessing a "heavenly glory," mortals putting on immortality, with impeachable beauty and radiance (1 Corinthians 15:35 – 41, 53). Our bodies will fit in nicely with the world to come.

The end of the Bible describes a day when everything is made new. John, one of the first followers of Jesus, describes this future day like this:

> And I saw the holy city ... coming down out of heaven from God, prepared as a bride adorned for her husband.

And I heard a loud voice from the throne saying, "Behold, the dwelling place of God is with man. He will dwell with them, and they will be his people, and God himself will be with them as their God. He will wipe away every tear from their eyes, and death shall be no more, neither shall there be mourning, nor crying, nor pain anymore, for the former things have passed away. (Revelation 21:2–4)

This is the day when God literally dwells with humanity. God will be present, not just with individuals, but with a whole new people. We will experience intimate, unhindered happiness in God's presence forever. As a people, we will face no more tears, death, mourning, or pain. All of those things will be gone. The resurrection began a chain of events that will lead to this future time, when everything will be as it should be. Today, we can live in light of that certain dream. The loud voice from the throne in this passage of Revelation is the voice of the resurrected Jesus.

This voice isn't just announcing a new relationship or new comforts. It announces: "Behold, I am making all things new" (Revelation 21:5). All things new! The resurrection affects everything. When Jesus rose from the dead to defeat sin, death, and evil, he overcame *everything* affected by the fall. Jesus is the first of a kind, not only a new kind of person but a new creation: "Then I saw a new heaven and a new earth" (Revelation 21:1). This is the promise of a new environment, no longer ruined by human exploitation. This is the promise of peace in a world that will no longer be ravaged by war. The resurrection of Christ is the teaser trailer of a whole new creation. His new corporeal quality is a foretase of things to come.

The Bible also tells us that the new creation is circumscribed with a holy city teeming with cultural life. The kings of the earth bring their cultural tribute into the kingdom to lie at the feet of King Jesus (Revelation 21:22–27; see also Isaiah 60). Some of the highest achievements of human culture are present in the new world. We should expect innovative technology, great works of art, and stunning architecture. Who knows? Perhaps we will have access to improved space (even time) travel, unhindered viewings of the Mona Lisa, and unrestricted access to Machu Picchu. Whatever it will be like, it will be truly awesome. The new creation will be populated by a resurrected people amidst a kaleidoscope of culture in the joyful service of King Jesus. This renewed creation is our future *and* our present. In Christ, God is *currently* making all things new. He is bringing the future into the present. How?

Where do we get the power to live such radical lives in the present, to be a bustling, creative, comforting, creation-renewing people? Where do we get the power to bring the future into the present? It comes from a powerful idea, an idea like the one described in the film *Inception*. This idea that "rewrites all the rules" is the idea of the gospel, the good news that Jesus has defeated sin, death, and evil *through his own death and resurrection* and is making all things new, even us. The power for a new creation comes through the one, true Human who remakes the world from the inside out.

In the resurrection, Jesus rolls the future back, a new creation, to start it right in the middle of history. He has begun the new creation. The power of the new creation is available to anyone who will receive it by faith. Jesus will take your old and give you new, remove your ugly and give you beauty, take your sin and give you righteousness, absorb your death and give you his life. This is the great hope of the gospel: "Therefore, if anyone is in Christ, he is a new creation. The old has passed away; behold, the new has come" (2 Corinthians 5:17). Now is new creation. The choice is ours, every single day: to believe the old or be the new. Will you live like Saito in *Inception*, dying an old man, filled with regret, waiting to die alone? Or will you take an informed "leap of faith" to believe in the resurrected Christ?

Hope, not sentiment, reminds us that we can rest each night knowing this day will come. It is a promise. As certain as the Sunday morning when the tomb was empty, there will be a day when God dwells with his people in a place without even the faintest hint of sin. We will rest in him forever.

Until then, those with resurrection life can persevere in giving, celebrating, and serving because we know we are part of a greater story. We continue on, even when there doesn't seem to be momentum or fruit, because we have joined the resurrection now. We remember that Jesus has been raised as a preview of the life to come. This is world-renewing resurrection.

When you are standing on the other side of the river, you know that resurrection life is worth believing in. You sense power in the mundane, a creative, life-changing power that resonates the closer you get to others. It motivates you to serve others for the flourishing of humanity. But at the center is a Person. You are now drawn into relationship with the most powerful, beautiful, creative Person in the universe—the risen Christ. The beloved disciple describes him:

> And in the midst of the lampstands [I saw] one like a son of man, clothed with a long robe and with a golden sash around his chest. The hairs of his head were white like wool, as white as snow. His eyes were like a flame of fire, his feet were like burnished bronze, refined in a furnace, and his voice was like the roar of many waters. In his right hand he held seven stars, from his mouth came a sharp two-edged sword, and his face was like the sun shining in full strength. (Revelation 1:13–16)

As we shared in chapter 1, the resurrection is like a river that seems impossible to cross when you first come to the riverbank. You can see the other side and it looks good, but you aren't sure how to get there. But there is a ferry there as well, subtly hidden off to the side. Will you take the ferry of faith across the river of doubt? Will you redirect your faith to the radiant Jesus? When you do, you are transported to the other side, through no doing of your own, right into the resurrection. Jesus carries you there, where you begin to experience the benefits of the resurrected life right away— a new authority (a gracious King), a new identity (truly human), and a new purpose (joining God in the renewal of all things).

By faith, Jesus' death and resurrection can become your death and resurrection, releasing you to live a truly human life. Best of all, when we turn away from trusting our unreliable selves to turn to the reliable, resurrected Christ, we gain intimacy with the most beautiful, powerful, creative, and gracious Person the world will ever know.

Life with Jesus is better. He offers deeper joy, more profound meaning, and true purpose. Life with Jesus is truer. He is the one we were made for. If you join Jesus, you will join the Person who changes everything, even us.

For Further Reading

Timothy Keller, *The Reason for God: Belief in an Age of Skepticism*. New York: Dutton, 2010.

T. D. Alexander, *Discovering Jesus: Why Four Gospels to Portray One Person*. Wheaton, IL: Crossway, 2010.

N. T. Wright, *Surprised by Hope: Rethinking Heaven, the Resurrection, and the Mission of the Church*. New York: HarperOne, 2008.

Lee Strobel, *The Case for Easter*. Grand Rapids: Zondervan, 2004.

Michael Goheen and Craig G. Bartholomew, *The Drama of Scripture: Finding our Place in the Biblical Story*. Grand Rapids: Baker Academic, 2004.

Eugene Peterson, *Living the Resurrection: The Risen Christ in Everyday Life*. Colorado Springs, CO: NavPress, 2006.

Stephen Smallman, *The Walk: Steps for New and Renewed Followers of Jesus*. Phillipsburg, NJ: Presbyterian and Reformed, 2009.

About the Authors

Jonathan K. Dodson is the founding pastor of City Life Church in Austin, Texas. He considers the remarkable claim that Jesus died and rose from the dead to be doubtful, essential, and pivotal for history. He holds a B.A. in Cultural Anthropology and two degrees in theology (M.Div and Th.M.) from Gordon-Conwell Seminary.

Brad Watson serves as a leader of *Bread&Wine Communities* in Portland, Oregon, where he develops and teaches leaders to form communities that love God and serve the city. He is passionate about helping people live lives that reflect their belief and hope in Jesus.

Notes

1. Barry A. Kosmin and Ariela Keysar, *American Religious Identity Survey (ARIS 2008)* (Hartford, CT: Trinity College, 2009); available at http://commons.trincoll.edu/aris/

2. "Now there was about this time Jesus, a wise man, if it be lawful to call him a man, for he was a doer of wonderful works, a teacher of such men as receive the truth with pleasure. He drew over to him both many of the Jews, and many of the Gentiles. He was the Christ; and when Pilate, at the suggestion of the principal men amongst us, had condemned him to the cross, those that loved him at the first did not forsake him, for he appeared to them alive again the third day, as the divine prophets had foretold these and ten thousand other wonderful things concerning him; and the tribe of Christians, so named from him, are not extinct to this day" (*Antiquities* 18.3.3).

3. For an insightful resource on skepticism and the claims of Christianity, see Timothy Keller's book, *The Reason for God: Belief in an Age of Skepticism* (New York: Dutton, 2010).

4. As someone who has struggled to makes sense of what may be competing or even fabricated accounts, I have found the writings of N. T. Wright and Richard Bauckham incredibly helpful. From shorter to lengthier works, see N. T. Wright, *Who Was Jesus?* (Grand Rapids: Eerdmans, 1993); *Jesus and the Victory of God* (Minneapolis: Fortress, 1999); and Richard Bauckham, *The Gospels for All Christians: Rethinking the Gospel Audiences* (Grand Rapids: Eerdmans, 1999); *Jesus and the Eyewitnesses: The Gospels as Eyewitness Testimony* (Grand Rapids: Eerdmans, 2008). A great

place to start is with T.D. Alexander's *Discovering Jesus: Why Four Gospels Portray One Person* (Wheaton, IL: Crossway, 2010).

5. I have adapted this metaphor from N.T. Wright, *Following Jesus* (Grand Rapids: Eerdmans, 1995), 110.

6. Philip Jenkins, *The Next Christendom: The Coming of Global Christianity* (New York: Oxford University Press, 2011).

7. Todd Johnson, "Christianity 2010: A View from the New *Atlas of Global Christianity*" *International Bulletin of Missionary Research* 34 (2010): 29–36.

8. Much of this historical reconstruction can be found in greater detail in N. T. Wright's tome, *The Resurrection of the Son of God* (Minneapolis: Fortress, 2003). Wright is arguably the foremost Jesus scholar alive today.

9. Arcade Fire, "My Body is a Cage," from the CD *Neon Bible*.

10. Wright, *Resurrection of the Son of God*, 82.

11. A full discussion of these themes can be found in Donald Gowan, *Eschatology in the Old Testament* (New York: T&T Clark, 2000).

12. Rodney Stark, *Cities of God: The Real Story of How Christianity Became an Urban Movement and Conquered Rome* (New York: HarperOne, 2007), 30.

13. Lee Strobel, *The Case for the Resurrection* (Grand Rapids: Zondervan, 2010) loc. 765 in Kindle book.

14. D.A. Carson notes six types of doubt: 1) Based on ignorance; 2) Based on systematic moral choice; 3) A rite of passage in solidifying belief; 4) Many little moral compromises; 5) By sleep deprivation (!); 6) By a personal existential crisis. Which form of doubt do you wrestle with? D.A. Carson, *Scandalous: The Cross and the Resurrection of Jesus* (Wheaton, IL: Crossway, 2010), 143-49.

15. I have borrowed this phrasing from Timothy Keller, *The Reason for God: Belief in an Age of Skepticism*, 211.

16. For a helpful book on a biblical view of heaven, we recommend Randy Alcorn, *Heaven* (Carol Stream, IL: Tyndale, 2004).

17. The section on "Renewed Future" is explained at the end of chapter 4.

18. The Bible does not record how creation came into existence. Whether it was by an evolutionary process or through divine fiat over literal days is not the author's concern. Rather, the main point of the creation story is to draw attention to God's sovereign creative power, the inherent goodness of the created order, and the unique place mankind holds in stewardship of creation.

19. See the following Scriptures: Genesis 3:15; 17:6; 49:10; Deuteronomy 18:5; 1 Samuel 2:10; 2 Samuel 7:12–14; Isaiah 52–53.

20. He continues: "One can only rationally doubt a statement on the basis of something else which one believes to be true. The critical principle destroys itself. If it is given primacy in the search for reliable knowledge, the end can only be total skepticism and nihilism." Lesslie Newbigin, *Lesslie Newbigin: Missionary Theologian: A Reader* (Grand Rapids: Eerdmans, 2006), 175.

21. I am by no means dismissing the valuable role of science. Scientific discoveries have overturned many stunning truths about our world. However, when the scientific viewpoint is taken as the arbiter of truth, we move from appreciating science to faith in science, which philosophers refer to as scientism or naturalism.

22. Eugene Peterson, *Practice Resurrection* (Grand Rapids: Eerdmans, 2010), 13–14.

23. Andrew Walls, *The Missionary Movement in Christian History* (Maryknoll, NY: Orbis, 1996), 51.

ZONDERVAN®